Developing Attitude Toward Learning

or SMATs 'n' SMUTs

Second Edition

Robert F. Mager

Lake Publishing Company
Belmont, California

BOOKS BY ROBERT F. MAGER

Preparing Instructional Objectives, *Revised Second Edition*

Measuring Instructional Results, *Second Edition*

Analyzing Performance Problems, *Second Edition*
(with Peter Pipe)

Goal Analysis, *Second Edition*

Developing Attitude Toward Learning, *Second Edition*

Making Instruction Work

Developing Vocational Instruction
(with Kenneth Beach)

Troubleshooting the Troubleshooting Course

Library of Congress Catalog Card Number: 83–60499
Printed in the United States of America

2.9

FOR

Albert Bandura, world's greatest SMATspert;

Maryjane Rees, magnificent manuscriptor's
midwife;

Peter Pipe, who held my hand from the beginning
(making it very difficult to type);

David Cram, who for the second time is being
referred to as Doctor Cram in print;

Ivan Zheesch, who will never be referred to as
Doctor Cram in print; and

Herschel Hirsute, who is seldom referred to at all.

There once was a teacher
Whose principal feature
Was hidden in quite an odd way.
    Students by millions
    Or possibly zillions
    Surrounded him all of the day.

When finally seen
By his scholarly dean
And asked how he managed the deed,
    He lifted three fingers
    And said, "All you swingers
    Need only to follow my lead.

"To rise from a zero
To Big Campus Hero,
To answer these questions you'll strive:
    Where am I going,
    How shall I get there, and
    How will I know I've arrived?"

Contents

Preface

ONCE UPON A TIME in a little drop of water, King Amoeba decided he wanted to teach his subjects how to have a better life. So he traveled far and wide throughout the Kingdom of Dropland to tell his people how to be better than they were. But nobody listened.

"Psst," said his advisor. "First you have to get their attention. Here. Rub on this magic garlic potion and you will get everyone's attention."

So the king did as he was told and went out to teach his people how to be better than they were. But nobody listened. They swam away . . . and held their noses.

"Psst," said his advisor. "You have to be sure they can hear you. Here. Shout into this megaphone and then everyone will listen."

So the king did as he was told, and went out to spread his wisdom. But nobody listened. They swam away . . . and held their noses . . . and covered their ears.

"Psst," said his advisor. "The people are too stupid to realize what wisdom you have to offer. You have to *make* them listen for their *own good*."

So the king made everyone gather in the Great Solarium while he told them how to be better than they were. But when the Great Doors were opened, everybody swam away so hard and so fast that before they knew it they had swum right out of Dropland. And henceforth and forevermore they were referred to as Outdroppers.

And the moral of this fable is that . . . *things surrounded by unpleasantness are seldom surrounded by people.*

There is no question that what we *teach* is often different from what we *tell*. Sometimes we teach the beauty and importance of a subject as well as the substance of it. Sometimes, though, we teach people to dislike, and then to avoid, the very subject we are teaching them about.

Developing Attitude Toward Learning is about a universal goal of instruction—the intent to send students away from instruction with at least as favorable an attitude toward the subjects taught as they had when they first arrived. It is about the conditions that influence this attitude, about how to recognize it, and about how to evaluate it.

This book is *not* about what to teach. It is simply about a way to help students get the best use of what they have been taught, and about how to influence them to learn more about your favorite subject after they have left you.

If you care whether your students use what you have taken the trouble to teach them, this book is for you.

ROBERT F. MAGER

Carefree, Arizona
January, 1984

PART

I

Where Am I Going?

1 | What It's All About

A thing, to be useful, has got to be used
But hated things, sir, are less used than abused.

People influence people. Since you are people, then *you* influence people. That's clear enough. But do you know just how you influence people? Do you know that you can have a great deal of control over the favorability of your influence?

That's what this book is all about. It is about some of the principles you can apply to positively influence your student's attitudes, about how you can find out how well you are doing, and about how you can find out how to do better. My sole intent is to aid you in sending students away from your instruction who are anxious to use what you have taught them—and eager to learn more.

Let's begin with a story.

A small boy of nine once looked forward to beginning his study of the violin. He admired his father, who played happy tunes on the violin, and he enjoyed music. His friends were studying various musical instruments, and he eagerly awaited the day he could call himself a musician. The day finally arrived, and, tucking his new violin under his arm, he started out toward an entirely new experience in learning.

What happened then? How did the story turn out?

A story like this could end in many ways. The boy might become a great violinist, enchanting millions with his skill. Or, lacking the talent of the virtuoso, he might become a very good violinist in a symphony orchestra. With even less talent, but continued interest, he might instead come to play the violin as a pleasurable hobby, providing enjoyment for himself and his friends.

On the other hand, he might come to hate the sound of the violin—perhaps even music itself—even with the talent to develop considerable skill.

Exactly how the story of an experience with an object or an activity *does* end is the result of the things that happen to a person while he or she is in the presence of that object or activity. The history of an attitude toward a subject is influenced by the events that occur in relation to it.

In the case of our small boy, the end of the story happens to be disappointing. Though he didn't have the talent to become a great violinist, he could, and did, make sufficient progress during four years of effort to enable him to make some very pleasant sounds. But alas, at that point he gave up the violin entirely and never played it again.

Why?

Surely *many* events could have influenced the gradual shaping of his attitude from positive to negative; *many* circumstances could have been responsible for the gradual strangulation of a willingness to learn and to use what had been learned. It may have been that the boy's friends made fun of him. It may have been the fact that the window of his "practicing" room faced the neighborhood baseball field, or that the violin was used as an instrument of punishment. ("You didn't come when I called you, so you have to practice an extra half hour.") It may even have been his teacher. Perhaps the teacher appeared continually angry at having to work with a "beginner," or showed nothing but dissatisfaction with the progress of this student. Perhaps the teacher always expected more than the boy could give. Or perhaps the student found himself being ridiculed or insulted by his teacher, or was in some other way made to fear the teacher.

Suppose our student had had a phenomenal talent for the violin. Would talent *alone* have assured an attitude favorable to continued association with the instrument? Would the student's talent have reached fruition even in the face of repeated ridicule, distractions, insensitive teaching, or constant punishment? Let me put it another way. Can you think of things that happened to cause people you know to dislike doing something they used to like to do? If so, you are confirming the fact that events influence people's attitudes. Although you may never know how these individuals might have behaved under different sets of circumstances, it is clear that both favorable and unfavorable circumstances influence behavior.

AND NOW?

One of the important goals of instruction is to prepare students to *use* the skills and knowledge they have learned and to prepare them to *learn more* about the subjects they have been taught. One way of reaching this goal is to send students away from the learning experience with a tendency to approach, rather than avoid, the subject of study. The remainder of this book is designed to help you achieve this goal.

2 | Why It's All About

If telling were the same as teaching, we'd all be so smart we could hardly stand it.

Why do we teach?

Why do we decide to construct a "course of instruction"?

What do we hope to achieve?

We instruct because we hope that through our instruction our students will somehow be different than they were before the instruction. We provide "learning experiences" with the intent that each student will then be a modified person . . . in knowledge, in attitude, in belief, in skill.

We teach in order to influence the capabilities of the student.

Consider any of the instruction you yourself may have given. Why did you coach, or tutor, or otherwise assist students to learn? Wasn't it because you hoped they would, as a result of your efforts,

- know more than they knew before?
- understand something they did not understand before?
- develop a skill that was not developed before?
- feel differently about a subject than they felt before?
- develop an appreciation for something where there was none before?

If your intent *was* to achieve one or more of these goals, then it was in these same ways that you hoped students would become different than they were before the instruction.

7

Many words are used to describe these intended differences. We talk about developing skills, or competencies, or
attitudes, or enthusiasm. We talk about encouraging growth,
about helping students to develop, or about assisting them to
develop to their fullest potential. Regardless of the words we
use to describe our teaching goals, and regardless of the goals,
*no teaching goal can be reached unless each student is
influenced to become different in some way than he or she was
before the instruction was undertaken.*

Equally important to reaching a teaching goal is timing.
When do we want the differences to appear?

Do we teach logic, and welding, and managing, and inter-
viewing only so that students can perform these skills *during*
the instruction, during the period of our influence?

Hardly.

We are far more concerned with influencing how students
are able to perform *after* the course is over, *after* our influence
is discontinued. We try to instill an appreciation for music *now*
so that students will behave appreciatively *after* our help has
been withdrawn. We try to teach them to read, to calculate, to
analyze *now* so that they will be able to do those things in the
future. And whether we are concerned with performance in the
immediate future or in the more remote future, we are concerned that our teaching influence become at least as evident
then as we want it to become evident *now*.

Dr. Jerome Bruner summarized the point exceedingly well:
"The first object of any act of learning . . . is that it should
serve us in the future."[1]

Certainly one of the important goals of education is that
the influence of an educational experience will extend beyond
the period of instruction.

My concern at this point is not with whether any particular
goal can be achieved through formal education, with whether

---

1. From *The Process of Education* by Jerome S. Bruner (Harvard
   University Press, Cambridge, Mass., 1960, p. 17).

it ought to be achieved, or even with whether it is stated in a way that facilitates achievement. My concern is only with noting that the actions implied by our instructional goals are expected to be performable at some time subsequent to the instruction—*at some time after the direct influence of the instructor has ended.*

There is nothing new about saying we are interested in having students use what we have taught them after instruction has ended, and the point may seem belabored. But if this goal is worth achieving, it is a goal worth doing more about than just talking. If it is a goal of value, we must act to achieve it, and act to learn how well we succeed.

So what?

Suppose it *is* true that instruction is intended to facilitate performance at some time after the instruction has taken place, you might ask. So what?

Just this. The more important your subject of instruction, the more important it is that students be *willing to use* what you have taught them. If you go to the great trouble of putting your own thoughts in order and organizing effective learning experiences for your students, you should certainly want to avoid the state of affairs implied by a graduate who says, "I hope I never hear of *that* subject again." What a waste that would be—of your talents and of the student's talents. You would have wasted *your* talents teaching someone something important that he or she will probably never use. The student would have wasted *his or her* talents learning (and then not using) a skill or knowledge that might have enabled him or her to be a little more successful, a little more useful, a little happier, or a little greater.

If it's worth teaching, isn't it worth working toward having that teaching put to use?

If one of our goals is to influence students to think about, learn about, talk about, and *do something about* our subject sometime after our direct influence over them comes to an end, how can we say we have been successful if students actively avoid any further mention of the subject?

Whatever else we do in the way of influencing students, the *least* we must strive to achieve is to send them away with favorable rather than unfavorable feelings about the subject or activity we teach. This might well be our minimum, and universal, goal in teaching.

(Of course, it isn't necessary for people to "like" a subject or activity in order for them to come into contact with it, or use it, or do something about it. Look at all the things people do that they would rather not do. Add up the time you spend doing things not of *your* choice. But this is just the point. People try to spend as much time as possible doing those things that they feel favorably about, and they avoid doing those things they feel unfavorably about . . . except when circumstances *prevent* them from doing so. Those who dread the thought of mathematics, for example, will struggle with some calculations . . . when they have to. Those who can't stand operatic music will sit through it . . . when there is no choice. When there *is* a choice, ex-students will be more likely to apply what we have taught them if they are favorably disposed toward the subject than if they hate the mention of it. And there *are* things we can do to accentuate the positive and eliminate the negative.)

Instructors, of course, don't control *all* of the factors that influence attitude toward learning. There are parents, there are peers, and there are neighborhoods. There are bosses, there are corporate policies, and there are laws. There is the uncle who was admired, and the aunt who was there to show the way. And then, of course, there is the mass media. So we must be realistic in our expectations.

But we can't pass the buck; we can't avoid facing the responsibility that flows from the fact that *we* influence attitude toward learning. The fact that there are other sources of influence doesn't alter the fact that instructors, as a group, constitute *one* of those sources. Since this is the case, it is up to each instructor to take whatever steps are available to assure that his or her influence is constructive rather than destructive.

SUMMARY SO FAR

- *Learning is for the* future; *that is, the object of instruction is to facilitate some form of behavior at a point* after *the instruction has been completed.*

- *The likelihood of students putting their knowledge to use is influenced by their* attitudes *for or against the subject. Things disliked have a way of being forgotten or avoided.*

- *People influence people. Teachers, and others,* do *influence attitudes toward subject matter—and toward learning itself.*

- *One goal toward which to strive is to have students leave your influence with their attitudes as favorable as possible toward your subject. In this way you will maximize the likelihood that students will use what they have learned and will be willing to learn more about what they have been taught.*

How to Proceed?

What can we actually *do* to help us accomplish the goal of sending students away with favorable attitudes toward what they have been taught? There are a number of things (otherwise, what's the point of writing all this?) that can be done. Happily, most of them will be within your power; that is, most of the actions that will improve student attitude toward learning will not require that you obtain someone's blessing or approval to initiate, will not require additional budget (money), and will not require additional equipment.

To know precisely the actions to take, however, requires that we know precisely the outcomes we hope to achieve. Just saying we want to achieve a favorable attitude is not enough. It's a good place to begin, but those words do not provide an accurate enough picture of the intended results to allow us to make decisions about *how* those results will be obtained.[2]

---

2. The process of analyzing goals into the components of their meaning is described in detail in *Goal Analysis, Second Edition,* by R. F. Mager (David S. Lake Pubishers, 1984).

The first step in our quest, therefore, will be to explore the matter of attitudes so that you will know how to recognize achievement of an attitude when you see it. We will define the goal we are hoping to achieve and then will consider the steps to be taken to improve our success.

3 ‖ Defining the Goal

If you're not sure where you're going, you're liable to end up someplace else.

Although goals such as "provide good customer service," "appreciate democracy," or "have a favorable attitude toward learning" may be laudable, they are difficult—if not impossible—to achieve when stated in such vague terms. Though these goals may *name* an important intention, they do not provide us with any information about what the intention would look like if achieved. And if we don't know what successful goal achievement looks like, we have no clues about what to do to accomplish that success. Before proceeding to action, therefore, we must spend a little time thinking about, and describing, the results the actions will be expected to achieve.

The first step is to consider the word "attitude." Although "attitude" is a useful word in everyday conversation—and I have used it myself earlier in this book—it is about as useful as a boot in a bedpan when we are serious about accomplishing an improvement in an attitude.

So let's think about attitude.

Is attitude a thing?

Wellll, no . . . attitude isn't a thing like a nose or a noose. You couldn't dissect a person's favorable attitude toward gumdrops and say, "Aha, madam. *There* is your attitude. Allow me to polish it up just a bit."

If attitude isn't a thing, what is it?

It's a word. Unfortunately, it's a word that has almost as many meanings as there are people using the word. But there is

13

some agreement about the meaning; no matter what the specifics of the meaning are, people who talk about an attitude are almost always talking about a tendency to behave in one way rather than in another. For example, if we note that a clump of people tend to say "Bleaaaugh!" whenever they are faced with limp string beans, we might conclude that they don't like limp string beans. We might say that they have an unfavorable attitude toward those mushy things. If we note that another gaggle of people tend to fall asleep shortly after the after-dinner speech begins, we might conclude that they have an unfavorable attitude about speakers. It is important to note that whenever we make such observations, we are making inferences about an alleged tendency *based on visible behavior*.

As a matter of fact, *all* statements about attitude are based on circumstantial evidence: on the evidence of what people say and do.

A good friend of mine has a favorable attitude toward Bach; that is, he likes to listen to music written by Bach. Now this statement is an inference on my part about a tendency, inclination, propensity—or "attitude." It is a conclusion about a general state of affairs based on circumstantial evidence. What kind of circumstantial evidence? Well, he talks about Bach whenever he can slip him into a conversation, and he frequently locates himself where the music of Bach is being played. And he does this for no reason at all . . . by which I mean there is no observable coercion—no visible or audible Bach stimuli to prod him. He simply makes numerous "moving toward" responses to Bach's music. So, from my observations I infer that he has a positive attitude toward Bach.

Attitude Statements Are Predictions. Whenever we make statements about attitudes, we are making predictions about the future behavior of people based on our observations of past behavior. Our predictions, or conclusions, may be right or wrong; but they are predictions nonetheless.

If we say that someone has a favorable attitude toward customers, for example, we predict that rather than avoid customers, this person would approach them, smile at them, ask how he or she may be helpful, provide assistance, and so on.

On the other hand, if we say that someone has a negative attitude about scorpions, we are predicting that this person would avoid the beasties whenever possible, would pass up opportunities to have one as a pet, and would say negative rather than positive things about scorpions.

When we tag someone as having a "favorable attitude," we are predicting some form of *moving toward* responses, and this prediction is based on some "moving toward" behavior already seen. Conversely, tagging a person as having a "negative attitude" is predicting *moving away from* responses, and that prediction is based on some "moving away from" behavior already observed.

Our quest, then, is to increase the strength of approach tendencies toward the subject and to minimize the strength of avoidance tendencies toward the subject; it is to cause the subject to become the object of "moving toward" behaviors rather than of "moving away from" behaviors. And now we can define our goal somewhat more precisely.

GOAL

To send students away with at least as strong an approach tendency toward the subject of _____ as they had when they arrived.

This means that no matter how much you teach your students, you will at least not do any harm to their interest in the subject. And as we now know, it also means that when the approach tendency toward the subject has been strengthened by increasing the ratio of approach to avoidance behaviors toward what is being taught, goal achievement will be accomplished.

THE NEXT STEP

The next step is clear. If we are going to increase the occurrence of approach behaviors and decrease the incidence of avoidance behaviors, we need to know what those are. Once we know exactly which behaviors we want more of and which we want less of, we can go about deciding how to get what we want.

4 | Recognizing Approach and Avoidance

A teacher with insight once turned
To a colleague and said, "I've discerned
That if I'm aversive
While waxing discursive
My students detest what they've learned."

"I'd rather be fishing," says one bumpersticker; "I'd rather be sailing," says another. Both are announcing a preference for one activity over others; both are announcing an approach tendency. Given a choice of activities, these bumperstick*ors* are telling us they would choose fishing and sailing. And the acts of obtaining and gluing the stickers to the bumpers are examples of approach responses.

APPROACH RESPONSES

An approach response is an action that indicates a *moving toward* an object, activity, or situation. It is a behavior that attempts to get the behaver closer to the target of the approach. It is a behavior that indicates an appreciation of the subject of the approach, whether that be sailing, mathematics, or asparagus.

There are three ways in which you could demonstrate an approach tendency. You could move physically toward the target, you could speak favorably about the target, or you could think favorably about the target. The first two are visible and qualify as approach behaviors. The third is invisible; and although favorable thinking and daydreaming about something are certainly real enough and certainly qualify as approach responses, they aren't usually thought of as visible behaviors. (Thank goodness! How else could we escape those dreary lectures?)

The world around us is filled with approach responses, and a little practice in observation will quickly enable you to spot them by the dozens. To get you started, let's consider some examples from a variety of areas.

First, let's take a look at a baseball fan. I'm sure you'll agree that fans have strong approach tendencies toward the target of their fanniness, and that they exhibit any number of behaviors indicating their liking of their favorite activity.

What tells you that someone likes baseball? What does he or she do that causes you to conclude that this person is nuts about the sport?

Suppose you were to observe a fan for a week, and suppose you were to record in your notebook everything he or she did that you consider evidence of a liking for baseball. At the end of the week, your notes might read something like this:

Talks incessantly about baseball.

Reads every word about the subject printed on the sports page of both local newspapers.

Can recite the batting averages of all players of all teams in both leagues.

During the observation week, watched every game telecast.

On Tuesday and Thursday, risked losing his or her job by calling in sick in order to attend doubleheaders.

On Friday, infuriated his or her spouse by watching baseball during a dinner party.

On Saturday, infuriated his or her spouse by spending the "dinner-out" money on the baseball pool.

This list by no means exhausts the possibilities. You will be astonished at the number of approach responses you will find once you begin to look for them. Some time ago, I ran into an excellent example of approach response toward this very subject. In a letter to one of the personal advice columns of the Chicago *Daily News,* a woman wrote:

> I know men are crazy about sports, but my husband carries this too far. He even took a transistor radio to his sister's wedding so he wouldn't miss the baseball game.

Clearly this man's behavior caused him to come closer to, or to remain in contact longer with, the subject of baseball; it is an approach response.

Next, consider the person who is known as an "opera enthusiast." If you were to observe and record this individual's behavior for a while to see what might have led to such a description, your notes might look something like this:

> Attends all local operas, regardless of cost.
> Talks about opera at length whenever possible.
> Tells nonenthusiasts that they "just don't know what they are missing."
> Reads books about opera.
> Frequently hums arias from various operas.
> Subscribes to an opera magazine.
> Owns an extensive record collection of favorite operas.

Again, the list of responses that represent an attempt to approach or remain in contact with opera has not been exhausted. Can you think of others?

Now let's look for approach responses more closely related to instruction. Here's an individual currently enrolled in the second semester of a college biology course. The student's instructor is frequently referred to as "enthusiastic," "inspiring," and "a good teacher." But you don't want to ask about the behavior of the instructor at this point. You are interested in the behavior of the student; more specifically, in discovering evidence from which to predict the nature of this student's future behavior toward the subject of biology. A week-long observation of this student might reveal the following:

During the week, student went to the library twelve times; used 70 percent of the time spent there reading biology books.

Tuesday evening, student attended meeting of the university biology club; broke date to attend.

Wednesday morning, spent $50.00 on biology texts and dissecting instruments.

Survey of attendance records shows that student has never missed a biology lecture or laboratory, but has cut two or three classes in each of several other courses.

During the week's three lectures and two laboratory periods, student asked 14 questions, all related to biology.

Asked to see the course instructor twice in office appointments to discuss points not covered in course.

On Thursday, student crouched on the banks of a river for three predawn hours to capture frogs for use as lab specimens.

Student met with advisor and asked to register for an advanced biology course.

You may object that this list contains exaggerations or that there are omissions, and you may not be willing to accept all the items as relevant to your own situation, but you will surely agree that it contains responses that can be used to make predictions (statements of approach or avoidance tendencies) about the student's future behavior toward biology.

The biology course just discussed had a lecture format. Let's look at a few of the approach responses commonly seen in courses operated according to a criterion-referenced, or competency-based, format. In these courses, students are given a copy of the course objectives so they know exactly what they must learn to do to be considered competent. They are given a variety of resources from which to learn and practice and are given a great deal of decision-making power over their own instruction. Instructors are available as coaches who assist in whatever way is needed to influence the learning to occur. Here are some of the approach behaviors you are likely to see in such a course setting. The students:

- fix work that is not yet adequate, without urging or pressure.
- spend time with colleagues (other students) discussing their work or reviewing the colleagues' work.
- complete more practice exercises than required.
- come early and stay late.
- sign up other people at their company for the course.

At one particular competency-based course in which managers and their subordinates learn some elements of modern management practice,[1] a number of students were so enthusiastic about what they were learning that they appointed themselves as a task force charged with implementing the techniques of management by objectives back at their organization. They held meetings on their own and developed an action plan. In addition, they drafted and rehearsed a presentation to be made to an executive vice-president upon their return to the company. Finally, they all asked their bosses to be allowed to become certified course managers (instructors) of the MBO course. Strong evidence of approach? You bet.

A word about "comes early/stays late" before moving on. Instructors of lecture courses often complain that students don't get to class on time. Instructors of self-paced, competency-based courses, on the other hand, often mumble about students who want to show up at 7:00 a.m. and don't want to leave at the end of the workshop day. In our own courses,[2] we have had to establish a policy of simply leaving the students at 4:30 p.m. and going to another room to complete our daily debriefing. Otherwise, we would have students who would still be working into the evening. This may sound unlikely to you if you have never experienced this form of instruction; I can

---

1. *Blueprint for MBO,* a workshop course on managing by objectives, created by Bonnie MacLean Abney (Abney & Associates, Burlingame, California, 1979).
2. *CRI (Criterion-Referenced Instruction): Analysis, Design, and Implementation, Second Edition,* an individualized workshop by R. F. Mager and Peter Pipe (Mager Associates, Carefree, Arizona, 1983).

assure you, however, that it is not an unusual experience for
those who operate their courses in this fashion. In Duluth,
Minnesota, for example, soon after the public schools went to
a competency-based format, teachers' complaints changed
from "We can't get them to show up on time" to "We can't get
them to go home in the afternoon." You understand the reason
for the complaint—if there are students on the premises, there
has to be an instructor there as well.

As you can see by these examples, people who are strongly
disposed toward a subject talk a great deal about it, encourage
others to participate in it, read about it, buy books about it,
study it, publish papers about it, and enter careers about it.
Students strongly disposed toward a subject sign up for more
courses about it, say favorable things about it, and spend time
practicing it.

In general, then, we can say that people with strong approach tendencies toward a subject keep coming back for more
experiences with the subject. They seek out experiences with
the subject in preference to other desirable experiences. *The
more strongly they are attracted to a subject, the more obstacles they will overcome to come into contact with it and stay in
contact with it.**

Identifying vs Weighing.   There is a difference between
recognizing a thing and putting a weight or value on it. It's one
thing to say "That's a stone," and another to say "That stone
weighs five pounds." The same is true for approach and avoidance responses. Identifying them is not the same as interpreting
and weighing them. Some are stronger indicators of approach,
or avoidance, and others are weaker. No matter, as long as you
remember that the goal is to maximize the incidence of approach behaviors and to minimize the incidence of avoidance
behaviors.

---

* One of the most interesting examples of an approach response was
this classified advertisement brought to my attention by Peter Pipe.

WANTED: Someone who watches *Love of Life* to fill in an episode
missed.

AVOIDANCE RESPONSES

Approach tendencies, however, are only half the story. There are also subjects that some people tend to avoid. If we can identify responses that lead us to conclude that a person tends toward a subject, we should also be able to identify responses indicating a person's tendency away from a subject.

Consider this pithy dialogue:

"Ahh, kiss me, you fool."
"Thank you, but I'd rather not."
"Why not?"
"I never kiss on Wednesdays."

It seems fairly obvious that the second speaker is trying to move away from the first speaker. This is an avoidance response, even though it is verbal. It does not matter *why* the behavior occurred. It doesn't matter whether it was because the first speaker suffered from bad breath or from crumpled toes. It doesn't matter whether it had anything to do with the attraction, or lack of it, of the second speaker for the first. If the response was "moving away from" behavior, it was an avoidance response.

Had you been observing and recording my behavior during the time I was working on the revision of this chapter, your notes might have looked something like this:

Turned on typewriter.
Got up to sharpen pencils.
Returned to chair.
Watched bunnies cavorting in desert outside window.
Typed half a page.
Watched covey of baby quail stroll by.
Got up to check thermometer.

Some of those responses look like approach responses and others like avoidance. Whatever my excuse or explanation, those that took me farther away from the typewriter can be called avoidance responses. (I dunno about you, but I find writing to be hard work.)

There are some subjects that may be avoided by people who actually "like" them very much. A fat person, for example, might manage to say "No, thank you" when offered a favorite dish, or an individual might avoid charging some coveted new clothes. These are special cases where someone avoids a subject in order to avoid an aversive (undesirable or disagreeable) consequence. The fat person avoids getting fatter and more uncomfortable (and possibly, avoids some stern comments from his or her physician); the individual hankering after the clothes avoids getting a bill that he or she can't afford to pay.

But what about matters closer to home—actions that might be used to infer an avoidance tendency toward an academic subject? The record of a student in his or her second semester of a required college mathematics course might look like this:

> On Tuesday, student tried to persuade mathematics instructor to excuse him or her from the course.
>
> Student failed to turn in three of four mathematics assignments on time.
>
> On Wednesday, student spoke with advisor about dropping out of mathematics course.
>
> On Monday and Wednesday, student was late for mathematics class; on Friday, student failed to appear.
>
> Discussion with instructor of first semester mathematics course revealed that student did not have the prerequisites necessary for the course and frequently complained that mathematics was unrelated to reality; instructor had evidence the student did very little studying.
>
> Discussion with student revealed that the person would be content if the subject was never mentioned again.

What other evidence of avoidance have you seen while attending someone else's course? Ever seen these? Ever seen the students:

- show up late?
- show up for class unprepared (no paper, no writing implements, etc.)?
- say unfavorable things about the subject of the course or about the instructional procedures?
- try to discourage others from signing up for the course?
- try to get by without practicing or studying?

What else can you add? What else have you seen people do, or heard them say, that suggested they would rather avoid contact with the subject or with the instruction itself?

The Origin of "SMATs 'n' SMUTs."   I had an opportunity to witness a hilarious assortment of avoidance behaviors during the original drafting of this book. Since the book was to be about Subject Matter Approach Tendencies, and in a way about Subject Matter Unapproach Tendencies, I referred to the book as "SMATs 'n' SMUTs." When my wife or kids would ask me what I was working on, I'd reply, "Oh, I'm trying to make some progress on 'SMATs 'n' SMUTs'."

As that became the "name" of the book around the house, I suggested it to the publisher as a title for the book. Well! You wouldn't believe the anguish this caused. Had you been watching, you would have heard and seen the following:

- Publisher recovers from shock and says, "There, there, now (pat, pat), that's a nice little joke . . . but you aren't *serious?*"
- Publisher suggests list of alternate titles.
- Editor says, "Well, let's see if it fits after we've worked through the rest of it," hoping it would go away.
- Editor launches into heartrending lament about the *Fanny Hill* implications of the title, and about how publishing people have a better "feel" for titles (and everything else) than authors.
- Editor melts into a little puddle.

In the face of such grief and pathos, I naturally gave up and settled for a phootnote. Imagine my surprise when, during the crafting of this second edition, the *editor* suggested that we use "SMATs 'n' SMUTs" as a subtitle. What had happened to cause the change of heart? The fact that catchy subtitles are used by readers more often than titles? An emboldening of the spirit? A mellowing of the psyche? Who cares? What matters is that the years have dissolved the avoidance tendency toward this silly subtitle, and now it is OK to try. My hat is off to this editor, who no longer puddles at the sight of my subtitles.

Meanwhile, back to the subject at hand. (Could I have been avoiding it?)

Given a choice, people with avoidance tendencies elect to approach something other than the subject in question. They will go to varying lengths to prevent contact with the subject. They do not buy or read books about the subject, they do not join clubs relating to the subject, and they do not seek out discussions concerning the subject. When they are faced with the subject, they act to move away from it by changing the topic of conversation, by walking away from the stimulus, or by inventing an excuse to avoid the subject or terminate contact with it.

More importantly, in instructional situations, people often verbalize a conviction that they cannot learn a particular subject matter and that they intend to have as little as possible to do with the subject in the future. *Once such a behavior pattern develops, it is unlikely that it will be reversed.*

To the extent students avoid experiences with a subject, they will have fewer opportunities to change their avoidance tendencies to approach tendencies. In addition, if students avoid experiences with a subject, it is improbable that they will use and maintain whatever skill they might have, and it is almost certain that they will learn little more about it as time goes by. Each subject students avoid constitutes the loss of a tool or skill that might have eased their journeys through a complex world.

It is for this reason that instruction that produces subject matter avoidance tendencies may very well do the student more harm than good.

(That good intentions are not enough was clearly demonstrated by an approach-avoidance analysis I conducted for a high school teacher of mathematics. This teacher is highly motivated to generate enthusiasm and appreciation for mathematics in her students. She likes what she teaches and is anxious that her students share her excitement for the subject. She is courteous and respectful of student questions and makes herself available for questions.

But in spite of her intentions and her initial success at motivation, she managed to *reduce* math interest in about as many students as she managed to increase it.

How? What could such a teacher be doing to diminish subject matter approach tendencies?

It was a classic example of "overkill." She inadvertently spent a great deal of class time presenting material beyond the ability of her students to understand. Her enthusiasm for her subject caused her to try to teach almost everything she knew about math, and that was a lot more than students could understand, regardless of how motivated they were to try. Some students concluded that they could never understand math, and they lost interest.)

THREE PROCEDURES

Here are three procedures that will help you to improve your ability to pinpoint approach and avoidance responses.

1. Think of something that your best friend likes, or dislikes, and ask yourself what that friend does or says that causes you to conclude that he or she has that like or dislike.

2. When you hear someone say something like "They have a poor attitude toward _____" or "They

are strongly motivated to _____," ask that person what it is that people say or do to trigger a comment about attitude or motivation.

3. Carry a small notebook and note each event that leads you to believe that a student is either favorably or unfavorably disposed toward the subject you are teaching. Don't worry that your list may include cats and dogs that don't belong there. They can always be culled later. Just try to get into the habits of observing and identifying clues to approach and avoidance.

Practice with these three procedures will prepare you to complete the first step, below, toward increasing student approach tendencies.

DESIRED PERFORMANCES

The first step toward improving students' approach tendencies is to draft a list of all the student performances you consider desirable. What would students be doing, and not doing, if they were learning and performing to your satisfaction? Write down each item; it is important to make a visible list, on paper, so you can more easily complete the steps that follow. Check each item on your list to decide if it is reasonable and makes sense; check to see whether the performance is now happening to your satisfaction; and finally, take steps to increase the frequency with which the desired performances occur.

What will such a list look like? What will people be doing, and not doing, if performing to your satisfaction? Do they:

- arrive prepared to work (i.e., with books, manuals, notebooks, pencils, or other equipment)?
- begin working on the instruction next in line for study?
- practice the material being learned?
- willingly correct work that is not yet adequate?
- speak favorably about the subject?
- ask for discussions about related aspects of the subject?

- ask questions when the instruction is unclear?
- do more work than necessary?
- discuss the subject with other students?
- spend time actually performing the skills being learned?

Flesh out your list over a period of a few days. Then go back over it to make sure that each item describes something you truly want students to do, and to make sure that your expectations are practical or realistic. For example, if you would be deluged and overworked if every student asked for extra work and then expected you to review the extra work promptly (there's no other way if you're a professional), you may have located an unrealistic expectation.

Once you have a visible picture of what you expect your students to do—whether that doing is related to approach/avoidance or something else—you will be ready to think about ways to accentuate the positive and eliminate the negative.

PART

II

How Shall
I Get There?

5 | Sources of Influence

If our actions didn't sometimes shout louder than our words, there would be no call for the expression, "Don't do as I do, do as I say."

A while ago, Von Haney, a talented graphic artist, created a short animation sequence for an instructional program designed to teach mothers something about the principles of behavior so that they might increase their success at interaction with those around them. In this sequence there are two small boys, one empty-handed and the other holding and sucking a huge lollipop. The empty-handed boy speaks first:

> "Hi. Where'd you get the sucker?"
> "My mommy gave it to me as a reward for crying."
> "You mean your mommy *wants* you to cry?"
> "I guess so. Whenever I cry she gives me a lollipop."
> "Gee, I'd cry a *lot* more often if I always got a sucker."
> "Of course. It's elementary psychology!"

Most people who have seen this sequence just *know* there was something wrong with the way the mother went about trying to reduce crying behavior, although they are often unable to put their finger on exactly what went awry. The sequence makes it seem obvious that crying behavior is not reduced by following it with a lollipop. But why not? Though the sequence doesn't tell us any of the details, it certainly does suggest that there are more successful and less successful ways of interacting with others, more successful and less successful ways of influencing others.

The business/industry version of the lollipop dialogue goes something like this:

33

"Hey! How'd you get the trip to Paris?"

"My boss gave it to me as a reward for screwing up."

"You mean your boss *wants* you to screw up?"

"I guess so. Every time my European operation doesn't meet its production schedules, she sends me to Paris."

Sound unlikely? Not at all. It happens every day; if not in these words, then in others.

"Charlie, you did such a good job on that report, I'm going to give you all the *tough* ones. You're just the man for the job."

Would anyone be surprised to hear that Charlie's lost his steam? That he seems less motivated than he used to? Suppose you had worked hard on an assignment and were then ignored when you presented the results. Worse, suppose you were asked, "Is *that* the best you can do?" Do you think that would affect how you went about completing the next assignment? Do you think your work would be affected if you never found out how well you were doing, or if you were in some way made to feel smaller as a result of your efforts?

The same holds true for students. They, too, are influenced by the things that happen to them. No one is exempt from the laws of behavior.

A few years ago a colleague and I implemented a study designed to chart the history of some tendencies toward, and away from, some academic subjects. We interviewed 65 students, currently enrolled in one course or another, who were all adults and who had completed high school and/or college.

The first questions of the interview were designed to identify the most favored and the least favored academic subject of each person. Once these subjects were identified, each person was asked a series of questions to determine just how these inclinations got to be that way. These questions were designed to explore each person's feelings about his or her most-preferred and least-preferred subjects, and to determine what the individual remembered as the conditions leading to those feelings and to changes in those feelings.

The results of the study were interesting and somewhat unexpected. Almost every person was able to identify the subjects or school activities that were at the top and at the bottom of his or her "popularity scale." What was unexpected were the responses to the questions attempting to discover why and how these subjects came to be rated as they were.

With regard to *favorite* academic subject, the interviewees seemed able to discuss the subject with some facility; that is, they talked as though they remembered something of the subject. But they seemed to have no clear idea of how it got to be their favorite subject. Though they always had an answer to the question "How did it get to be that way?" it was clear that their answers reflected only vague memories. "Oh, I always liked history," they would say, or "I was born with an interest in art."

When asked about the subject they liked least, the story was different. They seemed to remember little about the subject itself and would often come right out and say, "I don't remember a thing about _____ , and the less I hear of it the better." But they *always* remembered just how they learned to dislike the subject . . . at least they *said* they remembered. They were quite capable of pinpointing the events or conditions that they felt were behind their desire to avoid the subject whenever they could.

We were perfectly aware that some of the interviewees had faulty memories. What we were looking for, however, were the conditions and consequences they remembered as having an effect, whether or not they were correct, so we would know what they *said* to other people about the subjects they came to like and dislike.

As you read the sampling of interview summaries that follows, dip back into your own academic history to see if you can add other conditions and consequences that may influence approach and avoidance responses toward subjects taught in school.

Case 1

Favorite subject:	Music.
How it got that way:	I've always liked music. It was just a personal liking. No events had anything to do with it.
Least-favored subject:	English.
How it got that way:	None of the teachers could get down to a level where the students could understand what they were trying to get across. They didn't know how to make the subject interesting.

Case 2

Favorite subject:	Art, in high school; psychology, in college.
How it got that way:	I've always liked art. Mother encouraged art by providing lots of materials. In high school the instructor was very good. Had a good sense of humor, and worked *with* students. He encouraged us to participate in contests. I still use my art knowledge in my work.
Least-favored subject:	Mathematics.
How it got that way:	I was skipped to third grade after completing only half of second grade. I missed considerable background and felt lost. The third grade teacher was very impatient and did not believe in individual instruction. She ridiculed me in front of the class. I was above average in all other subjects, but I failed accounting in college.

Case 3

Favorite subject:	History.
How it got that way:	I hated math, wasn't good in English, and so, drifted into history. History interest continued through high school, which is as far as I went. I can't remember anything else that influenced my interest in history, but to this day I continue to study the subject as a hobby.
Least-favored subject:	Mathematics.
How it got that way:	I never could add 2 and 2, and still can't. I changed schools 18 times between first grade and the end of high school. Every time I got to a school, they were studying something for which I had no background, or they were learning something I already knew. Also, there was a grade school teacher who embarrassed me to death. The instructor once caught me counting on my fingers and took me up to the front of the class to make an example of me. It was humiliating.

Case 4

Favorite subject:	Spanish.
How it got that way:	High school instructor was tremendous; she spoke Spanish from the first day and taught class to sing Spanish songs. She encouraged special projects and allowed better students to help slower ones.

Least-favored subject: None. (No strong avoidance tendencies toward any subject. In college, this person majored in science. There were two reasons for this: (1) A cousin was taking science and interested the student by talking about it enthusiastically and by showing homework and experiments. (2) Student had a high school physiology teacher who had well-organized lectures and a good lab. This instructor checked lab work frequently and showed relevant films that were highly interesting. This instructor was a person to whom students felt they could go with problems. This is an instance where the attitude toward a subject changed over a period of time as the result of events and consequences.)

Case 5

Favorite subject: Psychology.

How it got that way: I had a great admiration for the instructor, and felt the course was well presented. He did not become angry when students disagreed with him . . . he was willing to be criticized. He did not ridicule. He encouraged his students and had no discipline problems.

Least-favored subject: Physics.

How it got that way: I felt I didn't have the mind for it. Also, I had a high school instructor I liked, but he merely read the textbook to the class and then assigned problems without giving the necessary information that would help in solving them. This instructor couldn't make himself understood.

Summarizing the results of this study, we can say that a favorite subject gets to be that way because the student:

- was comfortable in the presence of the subject.
- admired someone who was competent in the subject or who enjoyed demonstrating or working with the subject.
- found his or her world getting somehow brighter as a result of working with the subject.

A least favorite subject tends to get that way because the student:

- seems to have little aptitude for it (or feels that way).
- associates the subject with disliked individuals.
- associates the subject with unpleasant circumstances.
- found his or her world getting somehow dimmer as a result of contact with the subject.

There is no question about the fact that attitudes toward a subject are influenced by factors *other* than those present in the instructional environment. Peers, friends, bosses, and television are just a few of those factors. Our concern, though, is not with whether instructors are the *sole* source of influence, but with whether they are a *positive* source of influence. In other words, if a student is led toward an unfavorable attitude about something being taught, let it not be because of the actions of the instructor or because of the environment created by the instructor.

Try It—You'll Like It

Here's an activity that is always helpful in reminding us of the experiences that cause attitudes toward, and away from, a subject or activity. It follows the study described a page or two ago.

First, ask a friend to tell you what his or her favorite and least favorite school subjects were.

Second, ask if he or she can tell you how those school subjects got to be that way; that is, how the subjects came to be liked or disliked.

Third, ask if your friend has taken a course since starting his or her present job. Perhaps it was a three-day workshop, a seminar, or a longer course. If so, ask how your friend felt about that course or seminar.

Fourth, ask *why* your friend feels a particular way about this on-the-job course; that is, ask him or her to describe the events that shaped this attitude.

Finally, ask yourself this question: "What are the similarities and differences between the attitude-shaping events that occurred in school courses and those that occurred in courses taken while on the job?" Could the events leading to a less-than-positive attitude have been avoided?

SUMMARY

To summarize, sources of influence on tendencies to approach or avoid subject matter or activities include:

1. *The* conditions *that surround a subject or activity; that is, the conditions that exist while the student is in the presence of, or in contact with, the subject matter or activity.*

2. *The* consequences *of being in the presence of, or coming into contact with, the subject matter or activity; that is, the things that happen as a result of working with the subject.*

3. *The way that others react toward a subject; that is, the attitude* modeled *by others.*

Coming Attractions

Now that we have identified some of the sources of influence, the next step will be to explore just how these sources operate. We'll explore how they should be arranged in order to achieve a desired result.

6 Conditions and Consequences

Exhortation is used more and accomplishes less than almost any behavior-changing tool known to man.

The three types of events which, for our purposes, influence attitude toward learning are conditions, consequences, and modeling. So far, so good. But the nature of the conditions, the way in which consequences are organized, and the way in which the modeling is done make a difference. When principles are improperly applied, they don't work. Consider this improbable dialogue:

He: Y'know, I tried that gravity stuff.

She: You did?

He: Yeah. But it doesn't work.

She: What do you mean, it doesn't work?

He: See that there water trough?

She: Yes.

He: Well, the water is supposed to flow along there by gravity. But the principle of gravity just doesn't work.

She: Well of course it didn't work. You're trying to get gravity to make the water run uphill!

Odd, perhaps, but a way to illustrate the point that a principle is no less a principle just because it is misapplied. The principles governing human interaction are no different. Apply them correctly and they will work *for* you. Apply them incorrectly and they may work *against* you. So let's consider the correct and incorrect ways of applying the three types of events that influence attitude toward learning.

CONDITIONS

Whenever students are in the presence of the subject they are learning, they are also in the presence of conditions. There is temperature, which may be too cold or too hot, and there is furniture, which may be too hard or too soft. Furthermore, there is the psychological environment, which may be hostile and tense or pleasant and supportive.

When naturally unpleasant conditions are paired with a subject being learned—that is, when they are present at the same time—the thing being learned can eventually come to evoke approach or avoidance responses. That is, if a subject that initially has no special significance is presented to someone on several occasions while he or she is experiencing an aversive (unpleasant) condition, that subject may become a signal that triggers an avoidance response. Similarly, if a person is presented with a neutral subject and at the same time is in the presence of positive (pleasant) conditions, that subject may become a signal for an approach response.

Let's examine some everyday examples.

How do you react when a physician moves a hypodermic needle toward your arm? If you are like many people, you tend to back away; if you don't back away physically, you may turn your head to avoid seeing this signal for a forthcoming prick of pain. There is nothing aversive about the sight of the hypodermic needle—the first time you see one, that is. The needle is a neutral object. But after you have experienced aversive conditions (pain) while in the presence of a hypodermic needle, the needle itself becomes a signal for an avoidance response. It is as though the mere sight of a hypodermic needle becomes a condition to be avoided.

I came across this magnificent example in a letter that appeared in an Ann Landers column:

> . . . When my mother took me shopping, I soon learned not to express an opinion. My taste was "atrocious." Hers was "elegant." Once when I saw a dress I really wanted, my mother said, in the presence of the saleswoman, "You are as fat as a pig and that dress makes you look like a freak."

From then on I flatly refused to shop for clothes. I told my mother to bring home whatever she liked and I would wear it. I am a grown woman now, but these horrible memories are as vivid as if they had happened yesterday.

I hate clothes and I wear my dresses till they fall apart. *To this day, I cannot pass the dress section where we used to shop without being physically ill* [italics added].*

Yes, neutral subjects often turn into those that will attract or repel, and you will find many examples of them if you look around. You may not find many that result in the extreme reaction cited in the last example, but they are there nonetheless.

Going back to the study described earlier, there were several instances where the interviewees responded like this:

"At first I didn't care much about the subject one way or the other. But the instructor made me feel very comfortable, and I began to worry less about a grade and found myself studying the subject more intently than I had planned."

And like this:

"I didn't know what to expect when I first started in the course. But all the instructors were so cheerful, and seemed to delight so in the subject, that I soon found myself looking forward to learning more about it."

We see, then, that one way of ensuring that we are not the cause of an avoidance tendency toward the subject matter we teach is to arrange our instructional system so that when students are in the presence of the subject matter, they are, at the same time, (1) in the presence of positive conditions and (2) in the presence of as few aversive conditions as possible.

BUT. (There always seems to be a but in the ointment.) There is something else you must do to make this principle work for you. What?

---

* "Ann Landers" reprinted by permission of San Jose *Mercury* and Publishers-Hall Syndicate.

You need to make sure that the conditions are considered favorable or pleasant by the students you are instructing. Like trying to make water run uphill, the principle won't work if it is misapplied; if *you* are the only one who considers the conditions positive.

The rule, then, is this:

When in the presence of the subject you are teaching, students should at the same time be in the presence of conditions *they* consider positive or favorable, and in the presence of the fewest possible conditions *they* consider negative or unpleasant.

A Common Misconception.   Does application of this principle mean that instruction must be made "fun," and that students should not be required to work hard?

Not at all! Being in the presence of "work" is not necessarily the same as being in the presence of unpleasant conditions. Consider this dialogue:

"What kind of work do you do?"
"I'm in the sex business."
"The *what?*"
"The sex business. I teach actresses how to kiss."
"And you call that *work?*"
"It's not work, but it's a living."

This may seem an unlikely conversation, but it does serve to illustrate some of the confusion surrounding the word "work." This word has come to have several meanings. Sometimes it is used to refer to an occupation or profession, as in "What kind of work do you do?" When used this way, it seldom carries with it connotations of good or bad, pleasant or unpleasant. But *work* is also often used to refer to an activity that one would prefer to avoid, as in "Oh, that's work," or "I'd rather be enjoying myself, but I've got work to do." In these cases, the implication is that the activity referred to is one the speaker finds distasteful.

There is another way in which *work* is given a bad name. The familiar expression, "All work and no play makes Jack a dull boy," clearly implies that *play* is fun and *work* is not. What a horrible fate for a perfectly respectable word.

Were you to check your dictionary, you would find that *work* is "the expenditure of energy directed toward the accomplishment of something." It is engaging in some sort of purposeful activity. Skiing is work, swimming is work, playing the banjo is work, and so is writing. Haven't you ever engaged in purposeful activity that was exciting, engrossing, exhilarating, or just plain enjoyable? Haven't you ever heard anyone say, "I like my work?" Don't you like your work?

There must be something other than the expenditure of energy that causes the word "work" to have an aversive connotation with some activities and not with others. That something is the *conditions* associated with the activity, or the *consequences* following the activity.

> **When energy expenditure is associated with aversive conditions, that activity will tend to become aversive; when the energy expenditure is followed regularly by aversive consequences (punishment), that activity will tend to be avoided.**

There is nothing wrong with making students work. There is nothing wrong with making them work hard. But there are an infinite number of ways in which you can arrange the situation, *there are a lot of things you can do to them while they are working* . . . while they are in the presence of the subject you are teaching.

By all means make assignments, and by all means expect them to be carried out, on time. But also do your best to see that these activities are associated with positive conditions and with as few aversive conditions as possible. After all, even under the best of circumstances you will not cause everyone to be wild about your favorite subject. But professional practice demands that you do everything in your power to make certain you don't accidentally destroy whatever interest is already there. *Don't confuse work with unpleasantness.*

CONSEQUENCES

Imagine yourself a student again. When you correctly answer a question posed by your instructor, the instructor smiles and says something like "Good." When you answer a question incorrectly, the instructor makes a comment such as, "Well, let's look at the question again." Wouldn't the probability increase that you will be willing to answer questions and come into contact with the subject matter? In any case, this kind of interaction would not adversely influence your responses toward the subject. Conversely, suppose each time you answer a question incorrectly the instructor says, "Well I see old Dumbo is at it again." How long do you think it would be before you stopped raising your hand? How long do you think it would be before you began to think of excuses for not attending class?

When experience with a subject is *followed* by a positive (pleasant) consequence, the probability is increased that the subject will be approached again in the future. (Think for a moment about one or two people you like and ask yourself what there is about them that makes you want to be with them.) When, on the other hand, experience with a subject is followed by aversive (unpleasant) consequences, the probability is reduced that the subject will be approached in the future.

Consider this scene, taken from a practice film intended to help people learn to apply these principles.[1]

> *Worker:* Hey, boss! I've got the problem solved, and the production run will cost at least 30 percent less than we estimated.
>
> *Boss:* John, how many times do I have to ask you not to interrupt me while I'm working on budgets? . . . And will you please get that grubby apron cleaned?

---

1. *Who Did What to Whom—II?*, a film produced by Mager Associates, Inc. (Mager Associates, Carefree, Arizona, 1982).

As you can well imagine, the worker's shoulders sag as he walks out of the scene. Wouldn't yours? After this scene is shown, the following questions are asked. You might try to answer them yourself; then compare your responses with mine.

1. What happened to the worker who solved the problem? (Be careful here. The question asks you to describe the event, rather than to make an interpretation of the event.)

2. Will the worker be more, or less, likely to report his successes to the boss in the future?

3. How could the boss have handled the situation more successfully? (That is, what could the boss have said or done to have caused consequences considered positive by the worker?)

Check your responses on the next page.

1. He was criticized for interrupting and criticized for his appearance.

2. Less likely. His performance led to humiliation.

3. The boss could have:

   - said something nice about the solution.
   - paid attention to the worker's description of a successful experience.
   - asked questions about the solution (another way of rewarding with attention).
   - whooped and hollered with joy.
   - called others and told them the good news.
   - taken the worker to lunch.

   Can you add five more possibilities?

Though this film example dealt with the workplace, the same principles hold in the classroom. Consider this scene. A student walks into an instructor's office, and this interchange follows.

Stud: I turned in my extra project a week ago. That was the report that took 40 hours of library research and writing. I was wondering if you've had a chance yet to review it.

Inst: (Rummaging through a pile of papers on the desk.) Have you seen my calendar? (More rummaging.) I just don't understand why someone would take my calendar and not bring it back.

Stud: (Walks out of the office, head hanging low.)

Answer these questions about the interchange.

1. What happened to the student who asked for feedback? (Again, the question asks for events rather than for interpretation of the events.)

2. Did the student consider the events to be favorable or unfavorable?

3. How do you know?

4. Will the student be more or less likely to work that hard on a report in the future?

5. How might the instructor have handled the interaction more appropriately?

Turn the page to check your responses.

1. The student was ignored. The instructor spoke of things other than the report being asked about.

2. Unfavorable.

3. The student walked out of the office (avoidance response) with head hung low.

4. Less likely. Actions followed by unpleasantness are less likely to be repeated.

5. The instructor could have:
   - paid attention to the student.
   - said something favorable about the student's report.
   - asked questions about how the report was prepared.
   - smiled.
   - said something nice about the effort.

   Can you add a few more possibilities?

Positive consequences, then, make it more likely that students will become favorably disposed toward your subject, and negative or unpleasant (aversive) consequences will make it less likely.

But again we have a but. But there are two things you have to do to make the principle work for you. First, you have to *follow* the behavior with the consequence; the favorable consequence must come *after* the desired performance.

"All right. I'll give you the raise now, but you've just *got* to improve your accident record."

Lotsa luck! The correct application of this principle would look like this.

"First you improve your accident record, and *then* I'll give you the raise."

The second thing you have to do to make the principle work for you is similar to what you have to do for conditions—make sure that the consequences are considered favorable *by the students*. It isn't good enough that *you* get pleasure from the consequence; the students must also experience them as positive or desirable. "You did such a good job on that lesson that I'm going to tell you all about how I got started in this field" may provide you with a great deal of satisfaction, but what about the students? Do they care? Or would they consider your story to be an event to endure?

The rule for consequences, then, is this:

Follow subject matter contact with one or more consequences considered to be favorable by the students themselves.

This doesn't mean that you are expected to say or do something positive *each and every time* the students study or practice something. What it does mean is that the consequences should be positive rather than negative, and that contact with the subject should lead to the students' worlds getting somewhat brighter rather than somewhat dimmer.

Accentuate the positive and eliminate the negative.

Once again, the correct application of this principle does not imply that you refrain from making your students work hard. It *does* mean that the hard work should be followed by a ray of sunshine rather than by a bonk on the head.

ON TO SPECIFICS

The third way to increase the likelihood that you will send students away with a favorable attitude toward your subject is to model the performances you expect from your students. We'll consider modeling in Chapter 8.

Right now, let's think about exactly which conditions and events are positive and which are aversive.

7 | Positives and Aversives

People learn to avoid the things they are hit with.

Although it isn't always possible to know whether an event is positive or aversive for a given individual, some conditions and consequences are universal enough in their effect to provide considerable guidance. In this chapter we will examine some specific examples of positive and aversive conditions and consequences. Remembering that we're concerned with what is positive or aversive from the *students'* points of view, we'll begin with the negative. (That way we can end the chapter on a positive note.)

AVERSIVES

An *aversive condition or consequence* is any event that causes physical or mental discomfort. It is any event that causes a person to think less highly of himself or herself, that leads to a loss of self-respect or dignity, or that results in a strong anticipation of any of these. In general, any condition or consequence may be considered aversive if it causes a person to feel smaller or makes his or her world dimmer.

There are several conditions and consequences that are avoided by enough people to warrant their being referred to as *universal aversives*. When these conditions or consequences are associated with the subjects we teach or appear as a result of subject matter contact, then the subject matter, learning, or even the learning environment itself may take on a less desirable hue . . . and no amount of righteous indignation on our part will alter this effect, no declaiming of how the student "ought" to be more interested will have nearly as much effect toward that end as reducing the aversive characteristics of the learning situation.

Pain

is an acute physical discomfort, as you very well know. Though there are probably few situations left wherein instructors deliberately whop and bop their students, instructional pain is not yet extinct.

I know a violin instructor who, in an angry attempt to get his students' fingers properly positioned, makes those fingers hurt. He makes his students cry with pain and tremble with fear. His claim that this is "good" for the students is nothing more than justification for his uncommon version of educational malpractice.

We're talking here of pain inflicted by instructors as part of what they think to be "good instructional practice," rather than the kind of pain that may be an integral part of the subject matter. If you were learning to ride a horse, for example, you might experience a certain amount of pain in your . . . ah, well, backside. While that is a very real pain, it is horse-inflicted rather than instructor-inflicted. If you were learning to play football, you would experience a variety of kinds of pain that come from the game itself. If an instructor inflicts more pain than necessary to get the learning done, however, he or she is providing you with an example of primitive instructional practice.

When there *is* pain associated with learning the subject, instructors must go to greater pain (I just couldn't resist it) to counterbalance the aversives with positives. That is, instructors must try to make the learning experience net out as a positive one, by doing the kinds of things listed toward the end of this chapter.

Whether the pain is inflicted by the subject matter or by the instructor, pain is a condition people try to avoid. They do this either by learning to deal with the pain, or by leaving.

Fear and anxiety

are distress or uneasiness of the mind: apprehension of danger, misfortune, or pain; tension, stress, foreboding, worry, or disquiet; anticipation of the unpleasant.

Fear and anxiety are conditions that people try to avoid. When learning is associated with these states, the learner is more likely to learn to avoid the subject being taught.

Procedures leading to fear and anxiety are those that threaten various forms of unpleasantness. They include:

- Telling students by word or deed that nothing they can do will lead to success, or that contact with the subject will lead to undesirable consequences.
- Telling students, "You won't understand this, but. . . ."
- Telling students, "It ought to be perfectly obvious that. . . ."
- Threatening the exposure of "ignorance" by forcing individual students to solve problems in front of the class.
- Basing an attrition rate on administrative fiat rather than on student performance. ("Half of you won't be here a month from now," or "I don't believe in giving high grades.")
- Threatening failure by telling the student, "If you aren't motivated enough, you shouldn't be here." (*Translation:* "If you aren't motivated enough to learn in spite of my poor teaching, you certainly aren't going to get any help from me.")
- Being unpredictable about the standard of acceptable performance. (For example, a sixth grade teacher told his students that they didn't have to listen to his discussion if they were having no difficulty with its topic. Five minutes later he berated half the class for "not paying attention.")
- Being unpredictable about the standard of acceptable performance (by telling students one thing and then testing them on something else).

- Letting it be known that the students' general behavior will be reported back to their bosses at the end of the course.
- Basing evaluations on performance unrelated to the skills being taught. ("Oh sure, you learned it perfectly; but you seldom showed up on time, so I'm going to have to take ten points off for lateness." Or, "Oh sure, you learned to do it perfectly; but you took more practice swings than most other students.")
- Letting visitors sit in the back of the room.
- Evaluating students by comparing one against the other, rather than by comparing each with the criteria of acceptable performance established in advance.
- Creating stress unrelated to the learning, usually by making bizarre demands on classroom performance. ("Shine your shoes"; "sit up straight"; "pick up your pencil"; "put down your pencil"; "stand up and recite the table of random numbers"; etc.)

Frustration

is a condition or consequence that occurs when goal-directed activities are blocked, when purposeful or motivated activity is interfered with. To frustrate is to thwart, to foil, to circumvent, to interfere with, to check, to make an effort come to no avail, to nullify, to defeat. Practices that can generate frustration include:

- Presenting information in larger units, or at a faster pace, than a student can assimilate. (The more motivated a student is, the greater the frustration when his or her efforts are blocked.) A colleague describes this as the situation where a student came to drink from the fountain of knowledge and somebody turned on a fire hose.*
- Speaking too softly to be heard easily (blocking students' efforts to come into contact with the subject).

---

* Courtesy of Jack Vaughn.

- Keeping secret the intent of the instruction or the way in which performance will be evaluated.
- Providing unreadable print; type too small or too ornate, reading level too high.
- Providing obscure text, or implying more profundity than actually exists, as in, "When two parallel lines are cut by a transversal, the alternate interior angles are equal."
- Teaching one set of skills, and then testing for another.
- Testing for skills other than those stated in announced objectives.
- Refusing to answer student questions.
- Forcing all students to proceed at the same pace, thus frustrating the slow and boring the quick.
- Calling a halt when a student is absorbed with his or her instruction or attempting to complete a project (ringing a school bell, for example).
- Returning work to a student after an unusually long period (several hours or more), preventing the student from obtaining timely feedback on efforts expended.

Humiliation and embarrassment

are caused by lowering an individual's pride or self-respect, by making someone uncomfortably self-conscious; by shaming, debasing, or degrading someone; or by causing a person a painful loss of dignity. Procedures that lead to these conditions include:

- Publicly comparing a student unfavorably with others.
- Laughing at a student's efforts. When a colleague returned his comments on the original draft of this book, he included the following:

  My own pappy relates his music career thusly: "We had a singing session and the teacher asked me to sing alone. When I did, all the kids laughed. The next day he asked me to do it again. Well, sir, I wouldn't do it. So the teacher made me come to the front of the class, but I still wouldn't do it. So he hit my hand with a ruler. But he could have cut off my fingers and I *still* wouldn't have done it. I didn't, either. Ever!"*

- Spotlighting a student's weaknesses by bringing them to the attention of the class.

- Making a student wear a badge of his or her "stupidity" (putting him or her in a special seat or section, for example, or by requiring the student to keep the "dummy cup" on his or her desk until someone else "earns" the right to the same humiliation).

DENNIS the MENACE

"HOW COME I DON'T HAVE A SPECIAL PLACE TO SIT WHEN I DO SOMETHIN' **NICE** ?"

DENNIS THE MENACE® used by permission of Hank Ketcham and © by Field Enterprises, Inc.

- Belittling a student's attempt to approach the subject by such replies to his or her questions as "Stop trying to show off."

---

* Courtesy of Dr. David Cram.

- Insulting a student for his or her attempt to approach the subject by such comments as, "You couldn't possibly understand the answer to that question," or otherwise telling the student by word or deed that his or her questions are considered stupid.

- Repeated failure. It is perfectly appropriate to challenge students enough to cause them to fail on occasion, provided that the consequence of failure is not an avoidable aversive situation. Repeated failure, however, is sure to lead students to think less highly of themselves and to try to avoid the situations that have come to signify such a shrinkage of self-esteem. Repeated failure is often engineered into our educational system. One practice is that of grading on a curve. Whenever performances are evaluated by comparing them with what a number of chance neighbors happen to do, students with the below-average aptitudes will almost always come out on the lower half of the curve. They may have achieved all the objectives set out for them; they may have learned to work faster or more effectively; they may be exceeding the standard set out by the instructor. No matter. When their performances are compared with those of more talented neighbors, they will always be the losers. This use of the curve is only slightly less reprehensible than the instructor who brags that he or she has a "tough" course because 40 percent of the class "failed." (Has it ever occurred to the braggart that he or she is only 60 percent successful?)

- A common school practice leading to humiliation and embarrassment frequently occurs after a teacher has asked the class a question. In almost every class there seems to be at least one student who is so anxious to come into contact with the subject, so eager to demonstrate competence, that while frantically hand-waving for attention, he or she lets the answer slip out aloud. What is the consequence of this behavior? Does the student's world become a little brighter, is he or she encouraged to think more highly of himself or herself as a result of this action? Sometimes. Often, however, the consequence is a finger pointed sternly in the student's direction followed by, "I . . . didn't . . . call . . . on . . . you!" And what the student is learning is that it doesn't pay to get very excited about the things that happen in school, that showing too much interest can have unpleasant results, and that showing excitement can lead to embarrassment, to humiliation. Oh, I know. Students must be taught discipline (and discipline *will* be a problem as long as students are forced to sit in neat little rows listening to lectures). But there are better ways of handling discipline problems, ways that do not embarrass the student while in the presence of the subject matter.

Boredom

is caused by a situation in which the stimuli impinging on the student are weak, repetitive, or infrequent. Typical avoidance responses are those of leaving the situation and of falling asleep. Procedures leading to boredom include:

- Presenting information in a monotone.
- Rocking rhythmically back and forth while speaking.
- Insisting a student sit through instruction covering something that he or she already knows.
- Using impersonal, passive language.
- Providing information in increments so small that they provide no challenge or require no effort.
- Allowing lethargy-inducing temperatures to exist.
- Using only a single mode of presentation (no variety).
- Reading the textbook aloud. Consider for a moment the effect on a student of the instructor whose principal technique is to read aloud from the textbook. If a student has prepared for the class by studying the assignment in the textbook, he or she is punished for this effort through the boredom of repetition in the classroom. How can the student avoid some of the boredom of this situation? Very simply, by not doing his or her textbook

assignments before coming to class. In this way, although the student may suffer through a dull reading of the textbook during the class hour, at least the material read will not be familiar. This is one situation where the student is rewarded for being less, rather than more, diligent. He or she is reinforced for disregarding the assignments of the instructor. Since this situation is one in which the student's act of entering the classroom is followed by an unpleasant event (boredom), and since people tend to avoid unpleasant events, the student will simply try to avoid attending class whenever possible. And why not? Are *you* eager to place yourself in a boring situation? (Wake up there!)

- Going over material in class that was assigned as pre-reading. Similar to reading the text aloud, this practice promotes boredom. If students do, in fact, follow the instructions to read or study something before attending a class, they are almost certain to be bored during the early portion of the class. This is because most instructors cater to those who may *not* have followed the instructions regarding prereading. They go over the material regardless of whether students need it, thereby creating boredom for those who did as they were told. (In other words, following the directions is punishing. Students quickly learn that this can be avoided by not doing the preclass assignment.)

Physical discomfort

is an uneasiness, a hardship, mild pain. Though there are several ways of inducing physical discomfort while the student is in the presence of a subject, many of them are not under the direct control of the instructor. A partial list would include:

- Allowing excessive noise or other distractions, such as calling students from the classroom to put out "brush-fires" back at the office, allowing students to be interrupted by telephone calls, or requiring students to sit

through "guest lectures" unrelated to the purpose of the
course.

- Preventing students from moving around at will and
  from taking care of their personal needs (bathroom,
  toothache, headache, etc.).
- Requiring students to sit in those desk chairs that were
  obviously invented by a right-handed devil.
- Insisting that students be physically passive for longer
  periods of time than they can tolerate. (Here is an example of how discomfort, combined with a reward, led to a
  most unexpected result. A woman had a ten-year-old
  son who attended Sunday school with some reluctance.
  She wanted him to feel more positively toward church.
  The technique she selected for achieving this goal was to
  make the boy attend the *regular* service that followed
  the Sunday school session. The boy found the regular
  service a very uncomfortable affair indeed. He had to sit
  in a hard pew . . . he had to be quiet . . . he had to
  restrain himself from fidgeting. In addition, he was expected to listen to something he didn't understand at all.
  Since "sitting in church" was aversive, it was rewarding
  to leave church, because church-leaving led to a turning
  off of the discomfort. Result: Church became a symbol
  of discomfort and boredom and was avoided whenever
  possible.)
- Insisting that students pay close attention immediately
  after a meal.
- Making students travel farther between classrooms than
  can easily be accomplished in the time allotted.
- Making the classroom too hot or too cold.
- Requiring students to study under poor lighting conditions (such as is found in many hotel meeting rooms),
  leading to eyestrain and fatigue.

One school practice that produces aversive conditions and
consequences appears to be so common that I want to comment on it separately. This is the practice of using subject
matter as an instrument of punishment. You know how it

goes: "All right, because you were unruly you can just stay after school and work 25 arithmetic problems"; or "For that you can just read four chapters tonight instead of the one chapter I was going to assign." Again, the issue has nothing to do with the appropriateness or inappropriateness of punishment. It concerns only the *instrument* of punishment. People tend to avoid the things they are hit with, whether it be a club, a stick, or a subject matter assignment.

To keep herself from falling asleep while editing my manuscripts, the editor will sometimes actually think about the subject she is reading. As she read the previous paragraph she was kind enough to offer the following example.

"An instructor made an offender stay after class to do extra work, with the paper due at the end of the penalty session. Then, without looking at the paper, he tore it up in front of the student."

No doubt about it. When the subject matter itself is used as a form of punishment, students will quickly learn that the subject is something to be avoided.

So much for the negative side of the bench. Now let's consider the positive side, because that's where we'll find the payoff for improving attitude toward learning.

POSITIVES

A *positive condition or consequence* is any pleasant event that exists during the time the student is in the presence of the subject matter or that follows his or her approach to the subject matter. A positive condition or consequence causes the student to think a little more highly of himself or herself and causes the student's world to become a little brighter.

Conditions and consequences that are *universal positives* are just the opposite of the universal aversives. They are the events that lead to success experiences and acknowledge that success, ensure a variety of stimulation, lead to an increase of self-esteem or improved self-image, and lead to an increase in confidence. Positive practices include:

- Acknowledging students' responses, whether correct or incorrect, as attempts to learn, and following them with accepting rather than rejecting comments ("Try it again" rather than "How could anyone make such a stupid error!").
- Reinforcing or rewarding subject approach responses (a smile, a favorable word, a cheer, a cup of coffee or a lunch, or a little of your attention).
- Sending a student or three to look at a particularly good piece of work completed by another student.
- Providing a tangible token for successful completion of a particularly difficult or time-consuming piece of work. (In our workshops we literally use a large gold sticker, suitably imprinted for the occasion. Though a few of our students—adults—make pooh-pooh comments about the "gold star," they make sure they don't leave without it.)
- Providing instruction in increments that will allow success most of the time.
- Eliciting learning responses in private rather than in public.
- Providing enough signposts so that students always know where they are and where they're expected to go.
- Providing students with statements of your instructional objectives that they can understand when they first see them.
- Detecting what individual students already know, and then adjusting the curriculum in order to avoid boring individuals by teaching them what they already know.
- Providing feedback that is immediate and specific to a student's response.
- Giving students some choice in selecting and sequencing subject matter (especially where you maintain rigid control over the goals of the instruction), thus making positive involvement possible.

- Providing students with some control over the length of the instructional session.
- Relating new information to old, within the experience of each student.
- Treating students as individuals rather than as numbers in a faceless mass.
- Using active rather than passive words during presentations.
- Making use of those variables, such as motion, color, contrast, variety, and personal reference, known to be successful in attracting and holding human attention.
- For managers only: Allowing only those instructors who like and are enthusiastic about their subjects (and students) to teach.
- Making sure students can perform with ease, not just barely, so that confidence can be developed.
- Expressing genuine delight at seeing each student. (*Delighted* to see you again!)
- Expressing genuine delight at seeing a student succeed.
- Providing instructional tasks that are relevant to your objectives.
- Using only those test items relevant to your objectives.
- Allowing students to move about as freely as their physiology and their curiosity demand.

Going back to the study described in Chapter 5 again, here are some of the comments interviewees made about teacher practices they believed to have a positive influence on their interest in the subject under discussion:

"He taught us how to approach a problem so we could solve it for ourselves. He gave us the tools for learning."

"He broke the subject matter down into pieces we could understand. When we couldn't understand something, he tried to find another way of approaching it."

"He made books available at our level. That is, these were books that answered questions we had about the subject at that particular time."

"The instructor reinforced our desire to learn by giving us assistance and by showing a personal interest in what we were doing."

"He led discussions, but did not dominate them."

"He had a magnificent manner of presentation; he taught history as though it were a news analysis course, tying current happenings to historical happenings."

"He was always able to make individual students understand what was expected of them and where they stood."

"She used a lot of variety; she brought in other instructors, used films and demonstrations rather than pure lecture."

"He asked, and respected, the opinion of students . . . even though he didn't always agree with them."

"He knew his subject and always appeared to have time."

There is nothing revolutionary about the procedures listed in this chapter. Every instructor interested in increasing the capabilities of his or her students uses many or all of them, and others as well.

Then why go into such detail? Simply because *good intentions are not enough.* Though we are generally in favor of sending students away at least as interested in our subject as they were when they arrived, we do little or nothing to *ensure* that this is the case. Such apathy is frightening if one considers that the continuing use of factors leading to subject avoidance represents an enormous loss of potential skills. Those lost skills may well be one of the greatest burdens our economy will have to carry as we move into an age where a person without skills is virtually unemployable.

8 | Modeling

People see, people do.

Me:	If it is your desire that when instructing, your students confine themselves to an expository style of least complexity consistent with the subject matter and the target population, such an outcome is more probable of accomplishment if your own exposition is isomorphic to that which is desired.
You:	Huh?
Me:	If you want your students to use simple language when *they* teach, you should use simple language when *you* teach.
You:	Why didn't you say so?
Me:	I just did.
You:	Then how come you don't use simple language when *you* teach?
Me:	Don't do as I do, do as I say!

That silly little dialogue should serve to illustrate the essence of the modeling principles, which is—practice what you preach.

While it's true that we learn by practicing, by doing, and by being rewarded for our progress, it is also true that most of what we learn is learned by imitation. Most of what we learn comes from watching others do things that we then become able to do—or encouraged to do. When we see others do something, there is a tendency for us to imitate their actions. People see, people do.

This means that attitude toward (or away from) learning is strongly influenced by modeling. How does it work?

69

Modeling influences people mainly by *informing* them of a way of doing something. When something is demonstrated by a model, the observer is informed of a way in which that thing can be done. It may not be the right way or the desired way or the safe way, but the way shown is likely to be the way that is adopted.

Suppose you are vacationing overseas and a family asks you to have dinner. As you sit down to the meal you notice unfamiliar utensils alongside your plate. Since you don't know what they are for, what should you do? One appropriate way to react would be to ask what the utensils are for and how they are used. But it's more likely that you would watch to see what your host and hostess did and then follow suit, imitating the behavior that they modeled.

Fair enough. But how does this apply to a course? Well, have you ever had a course in which the instructor made unfavorable comments about the subject he or she was teaching?

"This is a required course, and I don't like it any better than you do."

"I don't know why I was assigned to teach this course, but I suppose we'd better get on with it."

"This is terribly uninteresting, but . . ."

"This is a dull film, but I'm supposed to show it."

It isn't easy to maintain one's enthusiasm in the face of comments like these. And have you ever attended a course in which the instructor just went through the motions of teaching—never smiled or said anything favorable about the subject being taught, simply recited old notes, and seemed as glad to leave the room as you were? Again, it's hard to maintain a favorable attitude toward anything when apathy is what is being modeled.

Would you know how to hold a knife if you wanted to kill someone? Sure you would. You saw it modeled on television. Would you know where to kick a man to put him out of business? Sure you would. You saw that modeled on television, too. You've seen a lot of things modeled there, things you now know how to do even though you will never do them. Why do you suppose influence groups try to stop programs from being shown on television? In part, it's because they don't want us to have certain attitudes modeled for us, because they don't want us to see how *others* behave toward one thing or another. They know that television is a powerful modeling medium, and that modeling changes behavior. (It's interesting that on the one hand the TV people try to convince us that television—and the sex and violence depicted there—*doesn't* influence people; on the other hand, TV people try to sell advertising by convincing their clients that TV *does* influence people.)

There are several principles of modeling. Some of these principles are listed here, along with an example or two to show you how each principle may be applied to the instructional environment.

1. Observers learn by watching and imitating others; they tend to behave as they have seen others behave.

   Application Example. Behave in the classroom the way you want others to behave. If you want students to observe certain safety precautions when handling equipment, then *you* observe those safety precautions.

   How *strongly* an observer will tend to imitate modeled performance is influenced by several factors. The following principles describe some of them.

2. Observers will be more likely to imitate a model who has prestige in the eyes of the observers.

   Application Example. Have desired performance demonstrated by someone your students respect: a manager, local hero, football player, or movie star. And don't forget that instructors often have prestige in the eyes of students, so it is doubly important that you practice what you teach.

3. Observers will be more likely to imitate modeled performance when they observe the model being reinforced for that performance.

Application Example. Arrange to have a demonstrator of desired performance (the model) applauded, awarded a trophy, given a raise, or praised—in the presence of the observers.

Application Example. A workshop participant offered this personal experience. "My own reports were always very descriptive (also long) until one day I heard my boss being congratulated for being concise in writing a one-page, fully satisfactory report. I now make it a point to be concise, too."

4. Observers who see a model being punished will tend not to imitate the performance that was punished.

Application Example. When someone is demonstrating correct performance, be sure he or she is not accidentally punished in the presence of the observers. Also, when participants do something wrong, be sure they are corrected; be sure they don't "get away" with it. (If the chief instructor cannot get away with parking in the president's parking place, the students will be less likely to try it.)

Application Example. (Also from a previous workshop participant.) "A colleague was told by our boss that he was too busy to see him. I have since had a tendency to wait until he calls me rather than try to make an appointment to see him. Ever since my colleague was 'put down' when trying to see the boss, I have tried to see him only on matters of utmost urgency."[1]

The research on modeling tells us that *if we would maximize subject matter approach tendencies in our students, we must exhibit those behaviors ourselves.* In other words, we must behave the way we want our students to behave.

---

1. Examples and other material in this chapter are taken from *CRI (Criterion-Referenced Instruction): Analysis, Design, and Implementation, Second Edition,* an individualized workshop by R. F. Mager and Peter Pipe (Mager Associates, Carefree, Arizona, 1983).

Although a display of interest and enthusiasm is not enough to guarantee that students will come to display similar feelings, the probability is certainly greater that this will happen than if we display apathy and disinterest. Conversely, a display of apathy on our part doesn't prevent a student from becoming more interested in our topics . . . but it doesn't help. Research has confirmed the fact that when you teach one thing and model something else, the teaching is less effective than if you practice what you teach.[2] The father, for example, whose approach is to say, "Stop fighting with the other kids or I'll whip you good," is less likely to be successful than if he were to model the kind of behavior he is interested in teaching. Parents are less likely to teach their kids to love their neighbor when the parents continually fight among themselves than if they were to model the behavior they want to teach. And, as Dr. Albert Bandura suggests, the father who exhorts his children to work hard in school, while he guzzles beer in front of the TV, is less likely to see the desired behavior than if he were to model the beaver instead of the sloth.[3]

What students learn by imitation, however, is not confined to their attitudes relating to various academic topics. For example, one professor who teaches psychology spends a great deal of time teaching students how to read and interpret journal articles. He teaches them how to recognize the difference between data and the interpretation of data and how to recognize the difference between adequate and inadequate controls. While doing this, he is also modeling a certain kind of behavior with regard to criticism. When a student condemns a research report because of a design flaw, this instructor says, "Perhaps. But what is the author trying to say? What is good about the

---

2. "Preaching and Practicing: Effects of Channel Discrepancy on Norm Internalization," an article by David Rosenhan, Frank Frederick, and Anne Burrowes in *Child Development,* Vol. 39, No. 1 (March 1968), pp. 291–301.
3. "Social Learning Through Imitation," an article by Albert Bandura in *Nebraska Symposium on Motivation: 1962* (M. R. Jones, ed.) (University of Nebraska Press, Lincoln, Nebraska, 1962), pp. 211–269.

study?" When a student is hypercritical because of the way in which a report is written, the instructor asks, "How could the author have said it better?" In other words, rather than model nit-picking criticism, this instructor models positive criticism, and it is likely his students will learn to do the same. If we would like to increase the frequency with which our students think critically or open-mindedly, we have a better chance of succeeding if we demonstrate these qualities ourselves. If we would have our students demonstrate a love for learning, we have a better chance of succeeding if we demonstrate that a quest for knowledge is more important than simple parroting of what is in the text.

Are we models worthy of imitation?

There's an easy way to find out. All you have to do is record one or two of your instructional sessions on videotape and then observe the results. (If you manage to sit through the entire playback without falling asleep, you can tell yourself you aren't too bad.) As you watch the playback, ask yourself these questions. Did you:

- spend time looking at the people you were talking to?
- use variety in your voice inflection (that is, avoid monotone)?
- smile when you talked, at least part of the time? (Do a "smile count." If you don't smile at least once every five minutes, you need some practice there.)
- say something positive about what you were teaching?
- say why others should find the topic of interest?
- refrain from hypnotic movements, such as swaying back and forth?
- refrain from negative comments, such as "This is sort of dull, but . . ."?
- refrain from stomping on students when *they* displayed interest in the subject?

There are some other things you can do to find out how successful you are in influencing attitude toward learning, and these will be considered in the next chapter.

WHERE ARE WE?

We have considered two of the ways in which behavior toward a subject may be influenced: by the conditions associated with subject matter approach and by the consequences of subject matter contact. In addition, some of the effects of modeling have been mentioned.

*There are other procedures that are more or less effective in influencing behavior, but a thorough discussion of each is beyond the scope of this book. I will only mention that ex-*hortation, *a procedure used regularly for centuries, has seldom been very successful in influencing behavior ("Pay close attention now, because in several weeks this material will become very important!"), and that the instructor who does little more than* insist *his or her students be interested, or* insist *they be motivated, will certainly have cause for complaining about student apathy.*

SMATs 'n' SMUTs, then, are influenced by the things we do and by the things we say ... whether we will it or not. To the extent that we come to recognize and apply those practices leading to approach behavior, we will come closer to reaching our objective of sending students away at least as favorably disposed toward our topic as they were when they came to us.

Now we'll consider ways of finding out how successful you are at achieving the SMAT objective.

PART

III

How Will I Know
I've Arrived?

9 | Evaluating Results

"You can't measure the effects of what I do."

"Why not?"

"They're intangible."

"Oh? Why should I pay you for intangible results?"

"Because I've been trained and licensed to practice."

"Hmm . . . all right. Here's your money."

"Where? I don't see it."

"Of course not . . . it's intangible."

Unless we act to evaluate our success in influencing subject matter approach tendencies, we can't substantiate any claims we might make in that direction. More importantly, we won't have as many clues as to how we might improve our efforts.

There are two kinds of evaluation to be considered. One is an assessment of whether our students appear to be as willing to approach our subject at the end of our influence as they were when it began (evaluation of results). The other is the assessment of how well we are applying the conditions and consequences principles described in the preceding chapters (evaluation of the potential for improvement of our results). In this chapter we'll deal with the evaluation of results; in the next chapter we'll think about how to improve those results.

Is Results Evaluation Difficult? At first glance, the problem of finding out whether our students are as interested in our subject at the end of the course as they were at the beginning seems insurmountable. If it were not so important, we might be tempted to give up before we began.

One reason the task seems so difficult is that there is not too much experience to draw on. Our teaching predecessors were not noted for the zeal with which they developed techniques to *measure* their success in influencing student "attitudes."

The problem, however, looks larger than it really is. After all, we are not concerned with hair-splitting measurements of tendency strengths; we are concerned only with discovering whether tendencies are positive or negative. We have enough work to do to eliminate the negative to worry too much at this point about fine gradations of tendency strengths.

There is another reason the problem isn't as large as it first appears. And that is that attitude evaluations are collections of information that will be used by yourself, privately. After all, since we (among others) are the ones who influence attitude, we are the ones who should be evaluated on our success at doing so. It isn't at all fair to grade students on whether or not they exhibit SMATs or SMUTs toward our favorite subject. It isn't fair for us to do things that stomp all over their attitudes, and then say, "Oh sure, you understand the subject perfectly; but your attitude isn't so hot and so I'll have to take ten points off." Therefore, since attitude assessments are really collections of feedback on how well *we* are doing, we don't have to be as precise as if we were publishing scholarly papers.

There is yet another reason why tendency evaluation is a manageable problem. Statements about tendencies are inferences or predictions based upon approach behaviors . . . and approach behaviors are quite tangible.

Since there is something to be learned from earlier attempts to measure so-called intangibles, we will begin there.

Where's Your Intelligence?   For many years, there was a serious search for what might be called the single-measure test of intelligence. Scientists measured the length of the forehead or the number and location of bumps on the head and tried to correlate their measurements with something called *intelligence*. But it was all in vain.

For one thing, there is no such "thing" as intelligence in the sense that there is a heart and a brain. Intelligence is not a structure or an organ that can be measured with a pair of calipers or a scale. Intelligence is a capability or capacity that cannot be accurately predicted by any *single* physical measurement.

Another reason the attempt to find the single-measure test of intelligence failed is that intelligence is a multifaceted characteristic that can only be inferred indirectly. That is to say, intelligence is a characteristic that is inferred from circumstantial evidence. It is a form of prediction about what a person would do, or about how skillfully he or she might handle a given situation, based on what a person has been seen to do.

Sometimes it's difficult to remember that the invention of a word, such as "intelligence," doesn't guarantee that there is a descriptive object to go with that word. I can invent a word like "bolguin," for example, or talk about "three-headed Martians," but that doesn't mean that bolguins and three-headed Martians really exist. Nor does it mean that other people will know what I'm talking about when I mention these words. I need to provide descriptions of "bolguin" and "three-headed Martian" in terms of the things I see them doing or saying.

If we want to define or measure an invisible characteristic such as "intelligence," we must first search for the items (behavior samples, a pattern of responses, and so forth) that might give us a more realistic prediction about the *nature* of the invisible characteristic. In other words, we must collect enough circumstantial evidence to enable us to accurately predict the characteristic's nature.

Like the trait "intelligence," "favorable attitude toward
_____" is an invisible characteristic. If we want to find
out whether students have a favorable attitude toward our
subject, we need to collect some items of evidence that will
indicate just what "favorable attitude toward _____" is
in terms of the things we want students to do or say in relation
to our subject.

There are two simple things we can do to collect the
evidence needed to get a handle on student attitude. We can (1)
ask students how they *feel* about our subject and then tally
their responses, and we can (2) observe what students are
actually *doing* as a result of their contact with our subject and
then tally the frequency of these student actions. Let's take a
closer look at these "How do they feel?" and "What are they
doing?" questions.

HOW DO THEY FEEL?

If I say to a student, "Hullo, there. How do you feel about
my subject?" and get a response of "Phffft," I know that all is
not well. On the other hand, if the response is "Gee, it's
terrific!" I can be more optimistic. I would want more evidence
than that one comment before concluding that this student has
a favorable attitude toward the subject, but it's a start.

The answer to the "How do you feel?" question can be
obtained with a questionnaire, offered at the beginning and/or
end of a course. If the questionnaire's indicators of attitude
move toward the positive, you will know you are on the right
track. What sorts of items should you use? Well, use (1) items
that ask students how they think they would behave when
placed in certain situations, (2) items that ask students to
rank-order their interest in your subject and other subjects,
and (3) items that ask students to make choices involving your
subject.

[Don't neglect direct questions. Sometimes the direct approach is quickest, least expensive, and most valid. Probably
the best way for me to find out whether you like pistachio nuts
is to come right out and ask you. If you say, "I like them very

much," I have better evidence from which to infer an approach tendency than if I had not asked such a direct question. We can learn a lot about people simply by asking them direct questions.

An experiment was once described to me that bears on the importance of the direct question. The military was reported to have conducted an experiment to find out how they could predict which soldiers would perform well in Arctic weather. They gave a large number of soldiers personality and aptitude tests, they measured blood pressure and other physiological variables, and they used questionnaires. After all the data were gathered, analyzed, and digested, they found that the best prognosticator of whether a man would function well in Arctic weather was simply to ask him "Do you like cold weather?" If the man replied "Heck, no!" it was a sure bet that he wouldn't do well in the Arctic.]

Some examples of questionnaire items are given on the following pages. As you read through them, remember that there are more of these sample questions here than you will need; four or five of the more appropriate ones would be enough.

Questionnaire Items

Since instructional environments differ in many ways, it is not possible to provide a complete questionnaire that will work in all situations. You will have to consider the items that follow as suggestions. Use the ones that apply, and derive your own from those that don't apply directly. Although the items are numbered consecutively, they are not listed in any order of importance.

1. Do you intend to take another course in _____ ?
   a. Yes.
   b. No.
   c. I'm not sure.

2. How interested are you in taking another course in _____ ?
   a. Very interested.
   b. Somewhat interested.
   c. I don't care one way or the other.
   d. Not too interested.
   e. Not at all interested.

3. How interested are you in learning more about _____ ?
   a. Very interested.
   b. Somewhat interested.
   c. I don't care one way or the other.
   d. Not too interested.
   e. Not at all interested.

4. If I had it to do all over again, I (would/would not) have taken this course.

5. I find the subject of _____
   a. Very interesting.
   b. Somewhat interesting.
   c. Somewhat uninteresting.
   d. Very uninteresting.

6. List all the subjects you are now taking and then rank-order them from most interesting to least interesting.

   [Leave adequate space for the answer.]

There are items (such as Items 7–11) that will bring the student more directly into contact with the subject. Since there may be a difference between what someone says and what he or she does, such "behavioral choice" items are useful. They come closer to requiring a commitment relating to the topic under discussion.

7. If someone suggested that you take up _____ as your life's work, what would you reply?

   _____

   _____

8. If you were asked to give a short talk about your favorite school subject, which subject would you talk about?

   _____

9. What would you reply if, in a casual group discussion, someone said, "_____ is very, very important, and everybody should try to learn as much about it as possible."

   _____

   _____

10. Write a paragraph about your favorite school subject.

    [Leave adequate space for the answer.]

11. Which of the following subjects would you be most interested in teaching?

    [List your subject and other subjects the student is studying.]

    a. _____
    b. _____
    c. _____
    d. _____

Another kind of item, generally called the adjective checklist, is shown in Item 12. It presents the student with a series of words that might express his or her opinions and asks the student to circle the words that do.

12. Circle each of the words that tell how you feel (mostly) about the subject of _____ .

fun	boring	too easy	too hard
useless	useful	exciting	interesting
essential	necessary	worthless	very important

Since it gives the student several quick opportunities to indicate a choice, an item modeled after the paired comparison may also be useful. It is simple to construct: (1) List your subject and three or four other subjects the student might be currently studying; (2) make a list of pairs of these subjects, pairing each subject once *with every other subject; (3) reverse the order of some of the pairs so that each subject is listed first about as many times as it is listed second; and (4) mix up the order of the items. With each subject paired at least once with every other subject, the student is asked to consider two subjects at a time and indicate a preference. A somewhat better index of the student's inclinations is thus gained than if he or she were to comment on each subject by itself. Instructions to the student may vary; they might ask which of the two subjects of a pair the student likes best, which of the two does he or she find more interesting, which of the two would be worth giving up a Saturday afternoon to learn more about, and so on. It is preferable to put each pair of subjects on a separate piece of paper, for later choices might be influenced by the pattern of earlier choices—the student might look back to make sure he or she is "consistent," for example. (A convenient way of handling this problem is to use narrow slips of paper, stapled on one side, with one pair of subjects on each slip.) Interpretation of this item is easy, since interest is confined to a single subject. For each student, count the number of times your subject has been circled. In the example in Item 13, each student could circle algebra from zero to three times. If there were 20 students in the class, algebra might be chosen from zero to 60 times, and the "score" might therefore range anywhere from zero to 60. If you administer the questionnaire at the beginning of your course and then during or at the end of your course, you can compare the results. If the second "score" is at least as large as the first, you might legitimately infer that attitude hasn't been impaired.*

13. On the slips of paper that follow, you are given pairs of subjects. Look at the pairs one at a time and draw a circle around the subject you personally find the more interesting of the two.

    1.   algebra   English

    2.   history   science

    3.   algebra   history

    4.   English   science

    5.   science   algebra

    6.   history   English

There is another behavioral-choice item you may be willing to use as one basis for predicting future behavior. The student is given pairs of paragraphs, each paragraph headed by the name of a subject and concerning some aspect of that subject. He or she is asked to pick one of the pair of paragraphs to read and to write a sentence about. (If you state a time limit as the student picks one of the pair, he or she may feel even more inclined to write a sentence about a favored topic.) An item like this, although similar to the previous pairing item, is different in that we are not merely asking the student to say which subject of the two is preferred, we are asking him or her to do something with the subject. Check your paragraph pairs to make sure there are no great differences between them; they should look alike on the printed page, be about the same length, and be as equally attractive as possible. (For example, if one paragraph contained dialogue and the other didn't, the eye might be quickly drawn to the dialogue. If one paragraph started out, "The early history of . . . ," and if the other began with, "Sex is the key to . . . ," or with, "Excitement is the only word for . . . ," they might be unevenly balanced in terms of attention-getting power. Finding paragraphs that might be suitable is not difficult; ask three or four students to select paragraphs that look about the same when there are no titles on them. The object of the item is to see which topics the student will select when given a choice . . . when all other things are equal except the subject.)

14. On the slips of paper that follow, you are given several pairs of paragraphs. As rapidly as you can, read *one* paragraph from each pair and write one sentence telling what the paragraph is about.

a.

ACCOUNTING

Good accounting practices can improve the efficiency with which a business functions. While providing accurate and current information about such things as accounts receivable and accounts payable, good accounting practices can also keep managers informed of other important items (inventory levels, money lost through bad debts, and so forth).

BUSINESS ENGLISH

The writing of business letters is one of the skills influencing the success of those who work in the business world. Those who write clear, understandable letters are much more likely to receive a favorable response than those whose letters are disorganized, full of strikeovers, or poor grammatically.

b.

SCIENCE

Although it is true that new facts and principles are the result of science, they are not science. Science is a process or a collection of processes through which new information and insight are developed. Scientists are scientists because of the procedures they follow in the pursuit of knowledge; they are not scientists because they know some of the results discovered by others.

HISTORY OF EDUCATION

It can be argued, then, that the introduction of the textbook into the American university was forced by the student and adjusted to by the administration. Students started many literary societies and read a great variety of books, and they learned from them. Textbooks were eventually introduced into classrooms as instructional aids, but with resistance from faculty and administration.

How long should a questionnaire be?

Your questionnaire should contain as many items as you feel are necessary to give you good evidence about the existence of approach or avoidance tendencies toward your subject.

Which items should a questionnaire include?

Those that *you* will accept; those that would cause you to make the instructional changes they suggest. Since you are constructing this instrument for your own use, it makes sense to include only those items that you will accept as meaningful. This is not to say you should not be interested in the *validity* of the items. After all, some items are better indicators than others of how a student is likely to behave in certain situations. But as important as the issue of validity is, I believe validity should be secondary to self-acceptance. *First* develop a set of indicators that you would accept, and *then* ask questions about validity. This way, you can get started *now* and refine your procedures as you gather experience.

> If students know we are asking "attitude" questions, can't they fake their responses? Aren't students merely going to tell us what they think we want to hear?

The honesty with which students will answer the items on a questionnaire partly depends on how well they trust the person who is doing the asking. If there is little trust, students will do their best to give what they think are appropriate answers; that is, answers that will do them as little damage as possible. If there is a great deal of trust, students will feel no need to conceal their true opinions, and they will be more likely to respond accurately.

Suppose I handed out a tendency questionnaire and said, "I am honestly interested in improving my instruction, and I would like very much to know whether I have succeeded in reaching some of my teaching objectives. I'd appreciate it if you would answer these questions as honestly as you can. Your answers will have nothing whatever to do with your grades."

And then suppose a small smile turned up my lips in gleeful anticipation. Would you believe my words or my lips?

There are any number of ways in which we can say one thing and clearly communicate something entirely different by our actions, but we *can* get reliable responses to questionnaire items if we ask for responses under appropriate conditions—conditions that convince students that we mean what we say.

If you have been an instructor for any length of time, you have probably developed some procedures for administering questionnaires to which there will be only anonymous responses. Perhaps you use items that require checking but no writing. Perhaps you ask a student to collect the papers and shuffle them before handing them to you. These are useful techniques, and you can easily collect others by asking your colleagues. The main thing is to arrange conditions so that students believe their responses will *in no way reflect on them or their grades.* Convincing them that there is no way in which you can identify their personal responses may be the best way to succeed. Insist that no names be put on papers, ask a student to collect papers and tabulate responses, ask that the questionnaire be answered outside the classroom and turned in to a student, or ask that papers be put into a box like a voter's ballot. Whatever procedure you select should indicate to your students your sincerity in wanting to improve the course.

As for instructions to students, I find that I get better results if I tell them I am trying to improve my instruction than if I tell them I am interested in measuring or assessing their attitudes about my subject. Students seem to be more eager to help in response to the first statement than to the second. I asked some students why this might be so, and their answers led me to conclude that it is because the statement "I want to learn something about your attitudes . . ." still has a hint of student grading in it.

If you decide to administer a questionnaire at the beginning of the course as well as at the end so you can see if there are positive or negative shifts in approach tendencies, I suggest you tell your students that their answers will help you make better decisions about how to organize the course and about where to put special emphasis.

WHAT ARE THEY DOING?

Asking people how they feel or how they think they would behave in certain situations is a legitimate way to collect information from which inferences about attitudes may be made. But the adage that says "actions speak louder than words" warrants some thought here. If I tell you that I like to read, and then you discover that I don't own any books, which would you believe—my words or my actions? If I tell you I think comic books are childish, and then you discover that my desk is full of them, would you put more weight on the words or the actions? Right.

So let's think about the kinds of actions that provide evidence of approach or avoidance toward your subject. Actually, there are two methods you could use to acquire your evidence; I'll describe them both, but I'll tell you up front that I much prefer the second one.

Identify All Possible Indicators

The first method involves listing all the indicators you can think of (whether approach or avoidance indicators), counting the frequency with which they occur, and drawing conclusions from the results. Here are some examples of the sorts of indicators you might use.

1. Percentage of students completing the course or total number of dropouts. (Of course there were good reasons for the dropouts, but the drop speaks louder than the excuse; dropping out is the extreme case of absenteeism.)
2. Total number of students late for class.
3. Total number of absences. (Industry has been using absenteeism as an indicator of approach tendencies for a long time.)
4. Total number of students choosing to attend an *optional* class session.
5. Number of projects completed that were *not* assigned or required.
6. Number of papers that were longer than required.

7. Number of reports more thoroughly researched than required.

8. Care with which projects were completed. (You might roughly categorize the products into three classes— neat, average, and sloppy—and keep a record of the number falling into each category.)

9. Number of assignments completed on time.

10. Number of students coming to your office to ask questions or to discuss the subject.

11. Number of students on time for their appointments with you.

12. Number of students electing to sign up for another course in the subject.

13. Number of students responding to a request for volunteers to work on a special subject-related project.

14. Number of unassigned library books taken out on the subject.

15. Amount of money spent by students for books, equipment, or materials relating to the subject. (How many classical records did they buy during the last 30 days of their music appreciation course?)

16. Total number of students active in a club or group organized in pursuit of the subject.

17. Number of students electing to make the subject the center of their life's work.

You will think of other possibilities, of course, but these will give you the idea. You can count the frequency with which these behaviors occur and make inferences about how well you are doing.

That's the first method. Here's the second.

Describe Desired Performance

Instead of counting all indicators (approach and avoidance) and then weighing the results of your count, I feel it is more productive to count only the indicators that describe what you want people to say or do. That is, instead of making a laundry list of all possible indicators, make a list of the performances you would like your students to exhibit. Then count the instances of those performances, without worrying about whether they are indicators of approach or of something else. This method asks you to say what you would take as evidence of success and then to look and see how well you are doing.

Here's how it's done. First, describe the things that you would expect students to say or do before you would be willing to say they have a favorable attitude toward your subject. Think of someone who does represent the attitude you seek, and list the performances that make you willing to say, "Now *there's* a person with a favorable attitude toward _____."

To help get you started, here's a composite list developed by others. Delete the items that don't apply, and add others that do. Make sure that when your list is finished you can say, "Yes. If students do or say these things, I would be willing to say they have a favorable attitude toward my subject."

Students:

- ask questions about the subject.
- come early and stay late.
- help other students learn the subject.
- say favorable things about the subject.
- read handouts during breaks.
- ask for more practice.
- ask for related courses.
- encourage others to sign up for the course.
- relate course content to their own job environments.
- do more than the minimum required.
- actually perform the skills being taught.

Again, never mind that some of the items would "fit" better under some category other than "favorable attitude." Just say what you want students to exhibit in the way of "desired performance."

When you have finished your draft, look to make sure that each item on the list is actually something you can see or hear someone do. Then ask yourself this question: "If someone did these things, would I be willing to say that he or she has a favorable attitude toward my subject?" If your answer is yes, then you are done listing performances. If your answer is no, then you will need to add the item or items that will cause you to answer in the affirmative.[1]

With this list of desired performances in hand, you are in a strong position to do two things.

1. You can determine whether or not each of these desired performances is occurring to your satisfaction. For example, if you want students to ask for more practice than is assigned, you can count the number who do that.

2. You can determine what to do to get more of what you want. Should you want students to ask questions when they are confused, for example, you can examine exactly what happens to students when they *do* ask questions (when they behave as you expect). If you discover that the students' world gets dimmer as a result of asking questions—that is, if they are punished when they perform the way you want them to—you can take steps to eliminate the source of punishment. In other words, you can carry out a performance analysis[2] to determine how to get more of what you want.

THERE MUST BE A HORSE IN HERE SOMEWHERE

(Just give me a moment to get my soapbox adjusted. Ahh, there.) What we have been up to in this chapter is considering ways to find out whether our students are or are not leaving with a favorable attitude toward what we are teaching. We've

---

1. For help with this procedure, see *Goal Analysis, Second Edition,* by R. F. Mager (David S. Lake Publishers, 1984).
2. This procedure is described and illustrated in *Analyzing Performance Problems, Second Edition,* by R. F. Mager and Peter Pipe (David S. Lake Publishers, 1984).

considered some methods that will help us acquire evidence, and we've had a chance to review some examples. Before moving to the next chapter, though, I'd like to put this in perspective.

If we are sincere about instructing as well as is possible, we will be interested in attitude as well as in content. That is, we will be interested in *shaping approach toward* the subject as well as in *teaching about* the subject. Further, we will be interested in finding out whether we are succeeding. No doubt about it.

So far, so good. But just how much time and effort does it really take to do this? In practice, not much at all. After all, we're not trying to measure something to the last molecule; we're simply trying to find out whether we are on the right track or whether we need to take action. That means thinking hard about what our expectations are in regard to student performance, finding out how well those expectations are being met, and then acting to improve the weak spots. All this can be done without mathematical knowledge (other than counting skills) and without the need for statistics. You don't need a scale that is accurate to a hundredth of a pound to tell you how skinny you are, and you don't need similarly refined measures to tell you how successful you are in sending people away with shiny attitudes.

So follow the steps outlined in this chapter, but don't lose sleep over the fact that your results won't be publishable in the *Psychological Journal of Wrinkled Attitudes* or that you haven't used the latest in statistical manipulations. It simply doesn't matter at all.

10 ‖ Improving Results

A poker player down to his last coins was asked, "How're ya doin'?"

"I dunno," he replied.

"What? You don't know how you're making out?"

"Oh, sure," said the player. "I know how I'm making out, but I don't know how I'm doing it."

If we knew what we were doing that was contributing to success, and if we knew what we were doing that was contributing to failure, we could do more of the one and less of the other. After all, we are dripping with good intentions and want only the best for our students. Sometimes, though, we know how well we are doing, but we don't know exactly how we are doing it or what to do to get more of it.

So this chapter is aimed at showing you how to review various components of your instruction in order to spot those components that may be acting to dampen the enthusiasm of your students. The purpose is to show you how to spot conditions and consequences that may have sneaked onto the scene without your knowing it. Once you know what they are, you will know what to do about them. You may not have the *clout* to do anything about them, but you will know what should be done about them.

AFFECT ANALYSIS

The procedure I'll be describing is one that reviews the emotional or "feeling" environment of your instruction and the things associated with that instruction. It has to do with analyzing those conditions and consequences that influence *affect*—that is, the approach/avoidance tendencies related to the subject you are teaching. It isn't difficult to do, but that doesn't make doing it any less important.

Specifically, the procedure asks you to answer three questions.

1. Are these obstacles that make it harder than necessary for students to come into contact with the subject?
2. Are there unpleasant or aversive conditions associated with *being* in contact with the subject?
3. Are there unpleasant or aversive consequences experienced by students as a *result* of coming into contact with your subject?

In other words, is it somehow difficult for students to get to the place where the subject is being taught, or difficult to get the materials they need? Is it somehow uncomfortable or humiliating to study the subject? And are students somehow made to feel smaller as a result of studying or performing the subject?

Sometimes the conditions and consequences that get in the way of more positive feelings toward the subject are easy to spot; actually, most are easy to spot once they are looked for. Occasionally, they are more devious. Here are some examples.

When I had occasion to teach Introductory Psychology more than 20 years ago, the other faculty members and I knew exactly what incoming students were interested in. They were interested in sex, in hypnotism, in ESP, and in the antics of the weird person down the hall of the dormitory. We knew all that. We talked about it, and we agreed on it. So how did we start the course? Did we tug on these interests and help them blossom to even greater heights? Did we fan these interests so that we could stimulate interest in other topics as well? Not for a minute! We started with the *history* of psychology. We bored the pants off these eager students with stories of the early eighteenth century, and about how . . . zzzzzzz. (Stop it! You're putting me to sleep.)

And then we would sit around in the faculty lounge complaining about the attitude of these students. Good grief. One should *never* begin teaching a subject to newcomers by teaching the history of the subject. That's the last thing students care about at that point. There's no *reason* for them to care. First, teach them something related to their interests; then, give them some competence in the area . . . along with feelings of competence. Do that, and then—because studying a subject's history is one way of fondling the subject, one way of getting closer to it—students may *become* interested in the subject's history.

A smashing example of the *right* way to begin a course was found in a locksmithing course I took by correspondence, after sending in an ad I found in a magazine. It was apparent that the developers of this course knew exactly why their students were taking this course, just as we knew why our students were taking our psychology courses. People were interested in knowing how to pick a lock. So guess where the course started. Right. Lesson 1 was on how to pick a lock. No history, no preamble; just a lesson on the subject most interesting *at that time* to the entering student. Nobody had to tell students that they weren't experts just because they knew how to pick one little lock; it was perfectly obvious. But oh, what a difference it made in attitude toward the subject! I was eager for the next lesson. Then I discovered that each set of five lessons came in a carton containing about two dozen numbered brown envelopes, about 2 × 3 inches, sealed. When, in the middle of a lesson, I was told "Now open Envelope 23," I would eagerly tear it open. Maybe it was only a key blank, or an allen wrench; but opening the envelope was as good as eating peanuts.

In fact, the course was laid out in such an attitude-enhancing manner that I found myself writing an irate letter to my instructor . . . because I had run out of lessons before the next batch had arrived. Now *that's* how to organize a course to improve attitude toward the subject.

But as I said earlier, it isn't always easy to spot the conditions or consequences acting against you (such as teaching the history of a subject before teaching the subject itself). I once had occasion to conduct an affect analysis for a teacher who couldn't understand the difficulty she was having in her class.

She was a fourth-grade art teacher who was very successful in motivating an interest in art activities. She was liked by her students, and they wanted to be able to do the things she could do. But by mid-semester it became clear that interest in art was declining. Many of the children demonstrated increasing apathy toward art and began expressing antagonism toward art class (not toward the teacher, but toward "art *class*"). An affect analysis for this teacher revealed the somewhat subtle cause of this situation. In explaining the project for the day, the teacher used between one-fourth to one-half of the class period. Then, just as the children had organized their materials and were hard at work, the bell rang and they had to stop and go on to another classroom.

There was good motivation in this case, and an enthusiastic and skillful teacher. But there was also an event that successfully blocked the motivated activity of the students . . . and frustration resulted. Since frustration is one of the conditions people try to avoid, these students came to associate art class with something unpleasant. Aggravating the situation still further was the fact that the teacher knew time was short, and this caused her to hover over the students while they worked and urge them to work faster.

Once this state of affairs was pointed out to the teacher, there was no need to suggest a solution; making her aware of it was enough. Although she had no control over the length of the period and could not change the administrative rules, she was able to get around the restrictive time allocation by reorganizing her activities so more work time would be available to the students.

WHAT TO OBSERVE

When hunting for conditions and consequences that may be getting in the way of a more favorable attitude, there are four general areas to explore:

1. The physical environment.
2. The instructional materials and devices.

3. The instructor.

4. The instructional procedures and policies.

Within each of these areas there are three categories of questions to answer.

Contact Difficulty.   How difficult is it for the student to make contact with the subject? How difficult is it for the student to experience the subject?

Contact Conditions.   How difficult is it for the student to stay in the presence of, or in contact with, the subject? What conditions associated with subject matter manipulation make it easy or difficult for the student to continue the activity?

Contact Consequences.   What are the consequences of working with the subject? What are the results of the student's attempts to learn and produce in relation to the subject?

The following material suggests some specific items to investigate or to observe in each of the four areas where conditions and consequences may be found. As you read these items, try to keep in mind that you may not be able to make all the changes indicated by your analysis as being necessary to make. Some changes may be beyond your power to initiate; some may be impractical or against policy. No matter. First you find 'em, and then you decide what to do about 'em. After you've finished reading these items, I will suggest a simple step-by-step procedure to follow as you do your sleuthing.

Physical Environment

Contact Difficulty.   How does the environment make it difficult for students to get into contact with the subject?

- Are the classrooms open during times when students prefer to study?
- Are computer terminals available when students need them or want them?

- How far do students have to go to get to the classroom? Is it easy for them to get there?
- Are students called away from the classroom?
- Can students easily *see* and *hear* the instruction?
- How good is the lighting?
- Do students have adequate work space?
- Is the environment too hot? Too cold? Too noisy? Too stuffy?

Contact Conditions. How does the physical environment make it easy or difficult to stay in contact with the learning task?

- Is the student work space relatively comfortable?
- Are students allowed to move around, or are they bolted to the floor in rows?
- Can students leave the classroom to take care of personal needs?
- Are there distractions? Noise? Activity?
- Is there tension, either deliberate or accidental?

Contact Consequences. How do students feel about leaving the learning environment? Does their world become brighter or dimmer?

- Are students anxious to leave the learning environment?
- Are students relieved when they leave the learning environment?
- Do students find excuses to leave the learning environment?

Instructional Materials and Devices

Contact Difficulty. Do the materials facilitate or inhibit student contact with the subject?

- Are there materials that help the student work with the subject, or is there nothing more than the instructor's words *about* the subject?

- Do type size and style make it difficult to read the material? (Ask a student.)
- Is the sound quality of audio materials good enough so that students can hear with ease?
- Is the material organized so that the student can easily find what he or she is looking for? Is it clearly indexed?
- Are the materials easy to get at?
- Can the projectors be operated easily? Extension cord available? Threading easy? Screen handy? Material clearly visible on screen without extensive room-darkening efforts?
- Are the computer terminals operational? Available?
- Are the videotapes stored in the classroom for easy access?
- Do the video playback machines work?
- Do the simulators work? Are they available?

Contact Conditions. How easy or difficult is it to continue to use the materials and devices?

- Does the equipment work reliably?
- When the equipment breaks down, is there someone there to repair it within a reasonable time?
- Are the instructional materials interesting or dull?
- Are the materials relevant to the learning objectives?
- Is it easy to see the place or importance of the materials, or do students consider them nuisances?
- What is the reading difficulty? (An introductory text was once prepared by a corporation for use in courses attended by individuals with a high school education. The text was well illustrated, comprehensive, and attractively bound. Some time after it had been distributed, however, it was found to be far too difficult for the students; the students couldn't get next to the ideas because of the vocabulary. Here was a case of freshman subject matter being taught with graduate school vocabulary. The discrepancy between subject matter level and

vocabulary level was "discovered" when it was found
that at least one group of instructors had written *another* text designed to teach the students to understand
the *introductory* text.)

- What is the viewing difficulty?
- What is the hearing difficulty?

Contact Consequences. What is the result of using the
course materials?

- Do students have eyestrain or headaches after difficult
  reading or viewing?
- Do students suffer from "relevance confusion"? Do they
  come away wondering why the materials were used?
- Are they exasperated or frustrated because of equipment
  malfunction?
- Are they frustrated because they had to watch while
  other students performed the experiments, made the
  adjustments, or took the measurements?

The Instructor

Contact Difficulty. What does the instructor do that
makes it easy or difficult for the students to experience the
subject? Does the instructor:

- Speak loud enough for all to hear easily?
- Speak clearly?
- Use a vocabulary level consistent with the subject level?
  (Does he or she use a freshman vocabulary for freshman
  subjects or a senior vocabulary for freshman subjects?)
- Continually orient students so that they always know
  where they are and where they are going?
- Specify instructional objectives clearly? Give students
  written copies of the objectives?
- Allow or encourage questions?
- Allow or encourage discussion? Allow each student to
  express and develop his or her own ideas?

- Allow or encourage students to pursue some special interest they may have developed in the subject? Or must they all follow the instructor?

Contact Conditions. What does the instructor do to make it easy or difficult to stay in contact with the subject? Does the instructor:

- Put students to sleep with a monotone?
- Read the textbook aloud?
- Lecture, and little else?
- Ramble?
- Appear to be interested or enthused about the subject? How much so?
- Require students to remain inactive for long periods of time?
- Show interest in teaching students, or is he or she more interested in keeping order?
- Behave as he or she wants each student to behave?
- Generate discomfort while talking about or presenting the subject? (One college instructor drops cigarette ashes on the students who are forced to sit in the front row. All eyes are on the ash, and it is very difficult to pay attention to the subject.)
- What happens while students are taking exams? Are they eager to demonstrate their achievement, or are they frightened and anxious?

Contact Consequences. What happens to students when they do work with, or manipulate, the target subject? Does the instructor:

- Answer student questions with interest? With hostility? With insult, ridicule, or disdain? Are student questions ignored?
- Respond to student comments or attempts to discuss the subject? How? Is the student made to feel stupid? Is he

or she encouraged or discouraged by the instructor's responses?

- Respond when a student completes a project or turns in an assignment? How?
- Return exam results promptly?
- Treat student work with respect, or hold the work up to ridicule?
- Insist that projects or assignments be evaluated promptly? By whom?
- Use subject matter as an instrument of punishment?
- Insist that assignments be turned in promptly, and then ignore them?
- Do anything that convinces the student that he or she could never be competent in the subject? That his or her best efforts aren't good enough?

Instructional Procedures and Policies

Contact Difficulty.   Are there rules or procedures that make it difficult for students to approach the subject?

- Are students required to show up at a certain time and prevented from studying before that time?
- Are all students expected to study the same thing at the same time and for the same length of time?
- Do the rules make it difficult for students to study a topic when they feel interested in it?
- Is the instructor accessible to the students when needed?
- Does distance get between students and the subject? How far do students have to travel between classroom and laboratory? Between classrooms?
- Are materials accessible to each student when he or she needs them?
- Is the library open when each student is free to use it?
- Are library books easily accessible to the student, or does the librarian stand between the student and the books?

- How much paperwork (form-filling) stands between the student and library books?
- How much administrative procedure stands between the instructor and course materials?
- Is equipment permanently available where students can use it?
- Are films, videotapes, and computer software permanently available where students can use them?
- Are students allowed to operate the equipment?
- Are visuals permanently available where the instructor uses them?
- What proportion of a period does the student spend in setting up and taking down equipment? In signing out and signing in?
- What proportion of the laboratory period does the student spend making calculations or doing other things that could as easily be done elsewhere?
- Does the instructor insist on checking every step of the student's work before he or she is allowed to proceed?
- What conditions exist that might discourage students from operating equipment and using materials?

Contact Conditions. Do the rules make it difficult for students to stay in contact with the subject?

- Are all students made to proceed at the same rate?
- Are brighter students prevented from "getting ahead" of slower students?
- Are slower students given more time to understand the subject and to achieve than other students?
- Are students to turn off their interest in one subject when a rigid time block ends (the bell rings) and turn on their interest in another subject? In other words, must student interest conform to administrative policy, or does policy encourage students to work with a subject until *they* reach a stopping point?

- Are classes frequently interrupted by announcements over a PA system or by other intrusions?
- Are students of considerably differing abilities paired, causing boredom to the faster and frustration or embarrassment to the slower?
- What conditions exist that make it difficult for the instructor to maintain interest in his or her students and in the subject?
- Is the instructor overloaded with busywork?

Contact Consequences.   Does administrative policy reward or punish students for their efforts?

- Are students who finish their work earlier than others made to sit still until others finish or until the period is over? Is their diligence followed by some other form of unpleasant consequence, such as cleaning chores or "make work" assignments?
- Are grades related to individual students' achievement in relation to course objectives, or to how well the students' peers happen to have performed? In other words, is evaluation based on objective-related performance?
- What kinds of recognition or privileges are there for student achievement?
- Do instructors hand out at least as many rewards as they do punishments?
- For what kinds of performance does management reward the instructors? Are instructors rewarded on the basis of their interest in, and efforts on behalf of, students? Are instructors rewarded on the basis of the amount of student behavior they have changed? Or are they rewarded mostly for committee work, publications, and the amount of equipment they display?
- Does administrative policy *allow* successful instructors to be rewarded more than unsuccessful ones?

- Does administrative policy reward unsuccessful teaching by taking from the classroom those students with whom the teacher has failed and giving them to specialists to work with in remote locations?
- What do managers *do* to identify how well each instructor is performing?

Each of the questions posed will provide a clue to one or more condition possibly operating to depress subject matter interest. They are by no means all the questions to ask, and do not identify all the things to look for. They provide a guide to get you started, and will, hopefully, remind you of other factors to check on.

While reading through the questions you may have had your doubts about the way they were organized . . . you may feel that one or more items should come under a different heading. Put them there. The object of the checklist is not to provide a neat classification system . . . the object is to provide an aid to the analysis of instructional effects.

HOW TO OBSERVE

1. Record one or two of your class sessions. Though videotaping is preferable because it provides more information, an audio recording is better than nothing. If your course has lab sessions, record one or two of them, too.
2. Play back the recordings in private while considering the questions that begin on page 101. Try to assume you are looking or listening to recordings taken in someone else's class. There is no need to get elaborate about the notes you take. After all, you are looking for clues to ways of increasing the percentage of approach responses, not in collecting data for a journal article. So keep it simple.
3. Spend some time looking over the materials used in the course. Inspect the texts, films, project materials,

and anything else that is used during instruction. If students are expected to operate equipment such as projectors and recorders, operate them yourself while asking the suggested questions.

4. Consider instructional procedures and policies in relation to their effect on your students. Consider the time of day that students study the subject, the length of the period, the difficulty of getting to the class from the previous one, administrative interruptions, and administrative rules that may affect approach.

5. Talk with a few of your students with a view toward checking the observations you have made during the previous steps. The students are the ones being influenced and, although their self-knowledge isn't perfect, their comments about their reactions are better than your guesses. If it is at all possible, talk with a few of the students who have completed the course under consideration. They may have a better idea about the durability of the effect of conditions that influence their interest.

ACTING ON OBSERVATIONS

What is the most aversive condition or consequence you have discovered? Is it under your direct control? If it is under your control, try to reduce or eliminate it. If it isn't under your control, it might be useful to bring the condition to the attention of the appropriate person. If the condition is not under your control and you judge it to be so much a part of the current system that you would have no chance of influencing it, it probably wouldn't help to mention it to anyone. Instead, try to find a way of working around it or minimizing it. For example, the aversive affects of an uncomfortable physical environment can be reduced by allowing students more freedom of movement.

Imagine that the notes you have taken are the results of an analysis of someone else's course, and that you are going to give the person a summary of the best and the worst of his or her instructional situation. Check those items in your notes. They are the items with which you should concern yourself. Ignore the rest. It is not easy to change, even for good causes; you are more likely to succeed if you concentrate on one item at a time.

It may come to pass that a colleague will ask you to help him or her with an analysis of his or her instruction and instructional environment. If this happens, and you accept, you have an obligation to report to *this* colleague, *and to no one else.* You should consider that you have contracted a client-counselor relationship; keep all results in the deepest confidence. If the person for whom you have made the observations wants to tell others about them . . . that is his or her prerogative . . . but it is not yours. In accepting a request to make observations and collect information, you agree to do just that—to make observations and collect information. It is highly inappropriate to pass judgment on your results by communicating it to others. Remember the wisdom that stems from the comment about casting the first stone, and about glass houses. Discretion is essential.

If you have never performed as a consultant before, one further word of caution is in order. Though your observations will be aimed at conditions relating to approach or avoidance, you will observe other things as well. You may very well observe events, procedures, or content not consistent with your own notions of effective instruction. Although it is inevitable that you *will* make such observations . . . *leave them alone.* Do not record them, do not talk about them, and do not report them to the person for whom you are observing. Even though this person has asked you to report on anything you think may be improved, it is unwise to include *everything* you observe. He or she is no more exempt from the laws of behavior than you or I, and one of the best ways of turning yourself into an aversive stimulus that your colleague will tend to avoid is to inundate him or her with criticism. Tell your "client" only about the conditions that may be affecting approach and avoidance behavior toward the subject. None of us likes to hear about our weaknesses . . . so be objective . . . and above all, be gentle. Do unto others. . . .

SUMMING UP

Our attitudes are influenced by the things that happen to us. When good things happen to us while in the presence of another person, we tend to feel more favorable toward that person. When we are made to feel smaller in the presence of that person, we tend to avoid future contact. The same is true for the subjects we teach. By neglecting student feeling, we can send them away with wrinkled attitudes toward our subject; we can send them away with a tendency to avoid the subject whenever they can. But by making sure that being in the presence of the subject makes them feel good about themselves, by making sure that the results of being in the presence of the subject make them feel good about themselves, by making sure that we model the enthusiasm we would like to encourage, we can send students away feeling good about what they were taught and showing eagerness to learn more.

It isn't difficult to do. And it's well worth doing.

Epilogue

It is easy to teach hate . . . anywhere in the world you look there is evidence of that. As a species, we do not seem to lack skill in teaching each other to avoid people of other colors, of other ideas, of other religions, and those who might have been born in this country or that. Perhaps there is something about us that makes this inevitable . . . perhaps we are not yet ready for a massive anti-hate program . . . perhaps we are not yet civilized enough, or strong enough, to apply what is already known in preventing further spread of aversion. Perhaps it isn't realistic for us to believe we are ready to try to stamp out the game of "you name it and I'll teach you to avoid it."

Perhaps.

Be that as it may, those with the responsibility for influencing the behavior of others cannot accept such a defeatist position. To be a professional means to accept responsibility . . . responsibility for actions and for results. It is to act in the best interests of those served . . . to help them grow rather than shrivel. When we accept the responsibility for professionally influencing the lives and actions of other people, we must do all we can to make that influence positive rather than negative. When we accept the money and the trust of the community, we must accept not only the responsibility for sending our students away with as much knowledge and skill as is within our power to give them, but also for sending them away with the ability and the inclination to use those skills to help themselves and others.

There are enough aversion-producing instruments in this old world of ours. As professional instructors, we must not let it be said that *we* are among them.

A Time
for Tribute

"Help, help," I cried.

And did they ever!

As you might guess, a book about approach tendencies ought to trigger approach responses toward the subject of approach responses. Accordingly, *Developing Attitude Toward Learning* was formulated in two loose stages. The first stage consisted of telling the content to members of the intended audience, individually and in groups, and noting their reactions, comments, and suggestions. The object was to find out what it took to get them nodding and to keep them nodding all the way through.

The second stage began when the content was in written form. It consisted mainly of asking instructors and colleagues who tested the various drafts to mark anything that slowed them down, turned them off, or rubbed them the wrong way; to describe what might have caused them to back off; and, finally, to describe what might have caused them to move forward.

And did they ever!

They made me change the sequence of topics until it made sense to *them*, and showed no respect whatever for what was "logical" to *me*; ripped out paragraphs I was very fond of and trampled them into oblivion; caused the demise of clever explanations that nobody seemed to understand; bludgeoned me into burning a long chapter (indeed!) on the development of affective objectives (there weren't any) and half of one on the statistics of attitude assessment (nobody cared); and vetoed examples that didn't examp.

Such impudence cannot go unpunished; such ego batterers must be exposed to public view. Therefore, with ropes of gratitude I tie to the pillory of immortality the 30 teachers who attended the workshop sponsored by the London County Council, the 20 teachers who attended a workshop sponsored by the University of Buffalo, the nine graduate student-teachers of the University of Rochester; and these more recent culprits, who made marks all over my neat pages: Albert Bandura; Bruce Bergum; Edith Bryant; David Cram; Anne Dreyfuss; Sister Charlene Foster, S.N.D. de Namur; Arthur Hyatt; Jane Kilkenny; Leon Lessinger; Richard Lewis; Jeanne Mager; Mike Nisos; Judy Opfer; Peter Pipe; Maryjane Rees; Charles Selden; Nancy Selden; Caroline Smiley; Margaret Steen; James Straubel; Walter Thorne; and Jack Vaughn. Especially in need of public exposure are those who offered their artistic opinion and witty remarks regarding the new cover design drafts. And those are these: Johan Adriaanse, Gérard Conesa, Paul Guersch, David Heath, Eileen Mager, Clair Miller, Fahad Omair, Dan Piskorik, Phil Postel, Jim Reed, Ethel Robinson, Bill Valen, Carol Valen, Bob White, and Letitia Wiley.